Once Upon a Calvary

the Cross, the Christ, the Criminals

Foye Adedokun

Kindle Direct Publishing

All Scripture quotations are taken from the King James Version (KJV), and World English Bible (WEB).

Once Upon a Calvary: the Cross, the Christ, the Criminals
Copyright © 2018 by Foye Adedokun
Published by Amazon Kindle Direct Publishers
Middleton, DE

Cover image by Foye Adedokun
Copyright © 2018 by Foye Adedokun

Printed in the United States of America.

Contents

In loving and cherished memory of Pastor Sam Farina.
"A wonderful man of God, a valiant soldier of Christ,
a true son of the Most High."
Pastor Sam, our family owes a lot to you, much more than you
knew before you slept. Sweet rest our pastor. Sweet rest.

Acknowledgments

✦ Thank You, Jesus, for Your death on Calvary. Though salvation costs sinners nothing to procure, it cost You everything to provide.

✦ Thank you, my enemy, for chasing me to Jesus. Though you meant to destroy my soul by refusing to back off. But God turned it around for my good when I ran to the cross, and there, I was saved.

✦ Thank you, dear reader, for this opportunity to be part of your life. You're my greatest inspiration. May the atoning death of our Savior continue to avail and prevail on your behalf. May you never regret picking up your cross to follow Christ, in Jesus' Name. Amen.

The Lord bless your reading of this book.
Thank you.
Foye Adedokun

And when he had called the people unto him with his disciples also, he said unto them, Whosoever will come after me, let him deny himself, and take up his cross, and follow me.
Mark 8:34

And whosoever doth not bear his cross, and come after me, cannot be my disciple.
Luke 14:27

Introduction

A cursed hill became a blessed hill because the One who turns curses into blessings was lifted up right there, just like He said before.

A day that broke with the light of a beautiful morning, soon turned into a day of sorrow and mourning. Mary was weeping, John was watching. Some were wailing, others were railing. It was supposed to be just another day, like thousands of days before it, except that an execution would be taking place, which wasn't an uncommon occurrence.

Villagers hurried past villagers—running, walking, paying no attention to one another. As the deaf raced past the lepers, the lame limped with vigor, determined not to be left behind. To the blind, the sound of feet marching past them, and the amount of dust blown into their nostrils, portended something unusual in the air. In groups of two, three, four, and more, people gathered on the hilly site called Golgotha. And by the looks on their faces, many couldn't put their fingers on the whole commotion. They seemed completely lost and puzzled. No doubt a unique event was taking place, but definitely not a joyful occasion.

Earlier on in the day, three crosses had touched down on

Calvary's top. Each one carried a man, hands and feet bound and nailed to it. It wasn't the first time criminals would climb that hill to their death. So why all the hullabaloo about that particular execution? In fact, anyone visiting the city for the first time would have thought there was a protest march going on. Well, in a way, there was, and the crowd seemed really divided between two sides—those for Christ versus those against Christ. As one side yelled, "Release Him," the other side yelled, "Crucify Him."

Obviously, it was an execution like no other, prompting the confused minds to ask questions from those flying to the site. And from the replies, many were not going there to watch the execution of the two real criminals, but that of the Man called Jesus—a just Man dying an unjust death. Who of the villagers wouldn't have heard about Him? He was popular and known all over the place as the miracle worker.

- At a wedding in Cana of Galilee, He turned water into wine (John 2:1-11).
- One day, in a city called Nain, He raised the dead son of a widow, the only child of his mother (Luke 7:11-15).
- On two different occasions, He fed a huge crowd with just a handful of food (Matthew 14:14-21; 15:32-38).
- Many people knew the popular crippled man in Jerusalem. For thirty-eight years, he missed an opportunity to be healed because he couldn't get inside the healing pool by himself, and no one

cared to help him, until Jesus healed him (John 5:1-9).

• To the man born blind, the crippled man had a better life. Though his condition hampered his movement, he could at least see and enjoy the beauty of light and day, and could tell the sun from the moon. For the blind man, it made no difference because he lived his life in total darkness, not knowing the next ditch he would fall into, or the next time he would run into a wall. His neighbors knew him as the man who "sat and begged," a title he had accepted as his fate.

But thank God for Jesus, who turned his darkness into light and restored sight to his eyes, a miracle that caused an uproar in the circle of the spiritually blind (John 9:1-41).

• Anybody from the country of Gadarenes would gladly tell you about how Jesus delivered them from the demoniac called Legion. His was a special case of lunacy. He "had his dwelling among the tombs; and no man could bind him, no, not with chains: Because that he had been often bound with fetters and chains, and the chains had been plucked asunder by him, and the fetters broken in pieces: neither could any man tame him. And always, night and day, he was in the mountains, and in the tombs, crying, and cutting himsclf with stoncs."

It's hard to imagine what the people who lived there had to put up with. But the day that guy encountered Jesus, he was made whole, a miracle he could not keep to himself. Like an undrafted disciple, he defied Jesus' order to "Go to your house, to your friends, and tell them what great things the Lord has done for you, and how he had mercy on you." Instead, he went and proclaimed it all over Decapolis (Mark 5:1-20).

- Can anyone deny the misery of the withered fig tree?

And Jesus entered into Jerusalem, and into the temple: and when he had looked round about upon all things, and now the eventide was come, he went out unto Bethany with the twelve. And on the morrow, when they were come from Bethany, he was hungry: And seeing a fig tree afar off having leaves, he came, if haply he might find any thing thereon: and when he came to it, he found nothing but leaves; for the time of figs was not yet. And Jesus answered and said unto it, No man eat fruit of thee hereafter for ever. And his disciples heard it. And when even was come, he went out of the city. And in the morning, as they passed by, they saw the fig tree dried up from the roots. And Peter calling to remembrance saith unto him, Master, behold, the fig tree which thou cursedst is withered away. And Jesus answering saith unto them, Have faith in God.
Mark 11:11-14, 19-22

If that tree were there today, it'll only be the dried skeleton of its original, just standing still for generations to see the tree on which Jesus placed the curse of barrenness.

- Yet, all those miracles pale in comparison to calling a dead and buried man out of his grave. Raising a dead person was enough wonder. But calling a dead man out of his grave? Never heard of until that day in Bethany, when Lazarus went from sick to dead and buried. But four days later, Jesus arrived at his grave. What happened next was time-freezing, as the Master over death commanded life back into a dead body. And with all eyes a gaze and all mouths agape, a four-day-old corpse walked out of his grave, turning him into a resented miracle among the Jews (John 11:1-44; 12:9-11).

Sometimes I wonder what really transpired inside that dark grave. Did he hear his name being called? Did he recognize the voice of the One asking him to come forth? Was he confused when he tried to open his eyes? Did he sneeze? Did he cough? Did he smell death, the smell of his own death? Any feelings of *rigor mortis* when he woke up? With him still "bound hand and foot with graveclothes: and his face was bound about with a napkin," how did he get up and walk out of the grave? Having spent four days in the grave, what kind of magic kept his body from decomposing?

And if he told of his four-day sojourn to the land of the dead, what tales would he tell? Did he see heaven, hell, or was he just floating around for four days? If he made it to heaven, what did he see? At what point was he asked to return to earth? On his way back, was he taken past hell fire, as some claim who have experienced astral trips (out-of-body experience)?

Those are the kind of questions I'll expect from people in their right minds. But for the chief priests, the miracle was more intimidating than it was awe-striking.

Of the four gospel accounts of Jesus' crucifixion, three refer to the site as Golgotha, and one refers to it as Calvary.

And when they were come unto a place called Golgotha, that is to say, a place of a skull, They gave him vinegar to drink mingled with gall: and when he had tasted thereof, he would not drink.
Matthew 27:33-34

And they bring him unto the place Golgotha, which is, being interpreted, The place of a skull. And they gave him to drink wine mingled with myrrh: but he received it not.
Mark 15:22-23

And he bearing his cross went forth into a place called the place of a skull, which is called in the Hebrew Golgotha: Where they crucified him, and two other with him, on either side one, and Jesus in the midst.
John 19:17-18

And when they were come to the place, which is called Calvary, there they crucified him, and the malefactors, one on the right hand, and the other on the left.
Luke 23:33

From the first three accounts, Golgotha means, *place of a skull,* suggesting a regular or popular site where criminals were executed, and their bodies were left to decompose until there was nothing left of them except their dried skulls and bones. The white-knuckle description makes it sound like a place of macabre that any sane mind would do anything to avoid. And it must have been a frightening hill to those living in and around the neighborhood.

The million-dollar question is not why did Jesus die on Calvary? But what crime did He commit to warrant a one-way trip to Golgotha, the same hill where hardened and vile criminals were executed? Why would a wonderful Man like Him be killed like a crook? If I let subjectivity control my feelings, I'll forever curse every hand that made Him go through such a terrible experience. But knowing that everything happened for a glorious reason makes it easier to be objectively emotional.

Like a beast of burden, Christ had to bear the sins of the world in His own body, so "that we, being dead to sins, should live unto righteousness" (1 Peter 2:24). Had He not been crucified, I would not have been saved.

―――――――――――――――――――――――――――――

With the number of executions carried out on Calvary, that hill must be doomed with the smell of death and damnation. But that was about to change because the Son of God would be lifted high on it.

And I, if I be lifted up from the earth, will draw all men unto me. This he said, signifying what death he should die.
John 12:32-33

As with anything in this life, when Christ comes on the scene, the story changes. Just give Him a chance to step into, or onto your situation, and watch Him turn your life into a spectacle of His miracle. That He did it before means He'll do it again.

- The day He rode a donkey to Jerusalem, that donkey received a royal welcome. "A very great multitude spread their garments in the way; others cut down branches from the trees, and strawed them in the way" (Matthew 21:8). Can you imagine how envious the other donkeys would be of their lucky donkey friend? It was because of Christ.

- In the Bible, there are six women named Mary. But one of them was highly favored above the rest because she carried and bore the Lord Jesus. Elizabeth—mother of John the Baptist— referred to her as "mother of my Lord" (Luke 1:39-44), such an honor that no other woman in history has been favored to have. A woman of low estate, no doubt. But from the time she carried the Lord in her womb, she became the "blessed" woman of every generation (Luke 1:48).

- Peter and his crew had gone fishing all night and caught nothing. As an experienced fisherman, if Peter caught nothing, it was because there was nothing to catch. Experience failed him, knowledge shamed him.

Distraught and disappointed, he and his crew got their things together, ready to return home empty-boated, or so they thought. They had no idea that a miracle was just around the corner, that their boat was about to experience a draught, a knowledge-and-experience-defying catch of fishes.

Now while the multitude pressed on him and heard the word of God, he was standing by the lake of Gennesaret. He saw two boats standing by the lake, but the fishermen had gone out of them, and were washing their nets. He entered into one of the boats, which was Simon's, and asked him to put out a little from the land. He sat down and taught the multitudes from the boat. When he had finished speaking, he said to Simon, "Put out into the deep, and let down your nets for a catch." Simon answered him, "Master, we worked all night, and took nothing; but at your word I will let down the net." When they had done this, they caught a great multitude of fish, and their net was breaking. And they beckoned unto their partners, which were in the other ship, that they should come and help them. And they came, and filled both the ships, so that they began to sink.
Luke 5:1-7, WEB

They were obviously exhausted and probably sleepy, just packing up to go home and rest. Then came a Man, whom Peter didn't recognize. The Man not only had the effrontery to ask to use Peter's boat for preaching, He also asked him to do what he already did all night with nothing to show for it. Thank God Peter didn't decline the Lord's request to use his boat, and also obeyed the Lord's command without questioning. Though already tired and disappointed, he entertained a stranger, not knowing he was entertaining the Lord. And because he didn't let his frustration control his emotion, what happened next blew his mind away.

Where were those scaly rascals when Peter wanted them? Or were they playing hide and seek with him? Hard to say. But the moment Jesus stepped into Peter's boat and began to speak, the fishes heard His voice from a distance away and raced back to the same spot where Peter and his crew had fruitlessly toiled all night.

Who says fishes can't recognize the voice of the Master when He speaks? Who says they can't sense the anointing? A special divine force must have driven those fishes back to that spot, and a whole lot more of them than Peter expected. At the Master's command to let his net down, Peter "nevertheless" obeyed and, boom, there they were, stampeding on themselves to make it inside the net of death. And if boats and nets could speak, they would be yelling—*Nooo!!! Stop!!! ¡Basta ya!!! Get ooooout*!!!

Speaking of an overflowing blessing, so much so that, not only did their nets break, even the boats of fellow fishermen were so full they all began to sink. It was a life-changing and faith-challenging moment for Peter. The toiling though lasted for the night, but the catching came in the morning because Jesus was involved. Because of Him, a night of nothing became a morning of overflowing.

He's the only One who turns emptiness into fullness and replaces lack with abundance. He reappoints the disappointed and transforms a nobody into somebody. He promotes the demoted and gives hope to the hopeless. He catapults individuals of low estate into blessed generations of great men and women. All He needs do is step into or onto, and everything would turn around for the best.

Calvary too didn't remain as that horrible hill because, on the day that Jesus stepped on it, its fate changed, forever. For the first and only time on that hill, the crucifixion of a "criminal" caused a three-hour daytime darkness over an entire land. The temple veil tore from top to bottom. His death made the earth to quake and the rocks to split. Even the centurion was so overtaken by awe, and he declared that Jesus was truly the Son of God.

And to bear greater testament to His supremacy, buried saints awoke from their sleep, took to "the holy city and appeared to many," like angelic ghosts.

Now from the sixth hour there was darkness over all the land until the ninth hour. Jesus cried again with a loud voice, and yielded up his spirit. Behold, the veil of the temple was torn in two from the top to the bottom. The earth quaked and the rocks were split. The tombs were opened, and many bodies of the saints who had fallen asleep were raised; and coming out of the tombs after his resurrection, they entered into the holy city and appeared to many. Now the centurion, and those who were with him watching Jesus, when they saw the earthquake, and the things that were done, feared exceedingly, saying, "Truly this was the Son of God."
Matthew 27:45, 50-54, WEB

The crucifixion of His Royal Majesty defeated the power of death and eternal damnation, and gave Calvary a new identity far from one of horror and terror. Today, ask anyone about Calvary or Golgotha. I doubt if the first response would be "place of a skull."

Everyone now remembers Calvary as the hill where Christ was crucified or the place where Jesus died for sinners.

In retrospect, any saved soul will see that day as the day of deliverance from bondage. But when we remember what Jesus endured to procure that deliverance for us, we get a better picture of what Calvary really means in the life of a true follower of Christ.

1

Calvary

And when they were come to the place, which is called Calvary,
there they crucified him, and the malefactors, one on the right
hand, and the other on the left.
Luke 23:33

Rewriting the history of Calvary (Golgotha) took more than the stroke of a pen, more so considering that it was only, and still is, the name of a hill. Though the hands of men played a major role in its sad mayhem, it took the sacrificial love of Christ to change the story of the "skull" site.

Before Christ's crucifixion, Golgotha stood as an epitome of horror, a place that anyone with a grain of integrity would avoid out of fear of shame and ridicule. But on the day that Christ was crucified there, a history of death unto damnation became a story of life unto salvation. From that moment forward, Calvary took up a new identity and ceased to be remembered as the hill filled with the stinking skulls and dried bones of criminals, long dead and forgotten.

There's no denying the fact that Calvary is synonymous

with agony, suffering, pain, and anything that a person has to endure once he (she) picks his (her) cross to follow Jesus. Whether we know it or not, and whether we admit it or not, everyone has a cross to carry and a Calvary to endure. Though Jesus suffered many things prior to Calvary, it was still the height of His suffering and the final destination, not to defeat, but to victory.

For believers in the Lord Jesus Christ, heaven marks the final victory over all the battles we'll fight before we get there. And as exciting as the Christian journey is, it's still an arduous and unpredictable journey. As children of God, we know that picking the cross means following Jesus. And we always hope that the journey is smooth, with no tales of trials and tribulations. Just pick the cross and make a smooth sail to heaven. Well, that may be so for some folks. But for others like me, the journey seems to have more bumps and hurdles than we're prepared for.

With that in mind, what lessons can we learn from Calvary to help us travel this Christian journey without giving up on the way? And what exactly does Calvary mean to anyone who decides to follow Christ?

Facts about Calvary

Road to Calvary is unpredictable

Before Jesus was born, there were prophecies about His birth, His place of birth, His virgin birth, His Names, and His Messiahship. There were equally many prophecies about what He would suffer as the Savior of the world.

• That He would be despised and rejected by men, and He would experience sorrows and suffering (Isaiah 53:3; John 1).

• That He would be beaten and spat upon (Isaiah 50:6; Matthew 26).

• That someone He trusted and shared bread with would lift up his heel against Him. Judas Iscariot betrayed Jesus (Psalm 41:9; Mark 14).

• That He would be led like a lamb to the slaughter; and He would remain silent in oppression and affliction. Pilate did everything to make Him speak, but Jesus remained silent (Isaiah 53:7; Mark 15).

• That in His agony, He would question His Father and cry, "My God, my God, why have you forsaken me?" On the cross, Jesus cried, "Eloi, Eloi, lama sabachthani?" It means, "My God, my God, why hast thou forsaken me?" (Psalm 22:1; Matthew 27).

• That He would be mocked and insulted by people who saw Him hanging on the cross and thought He "couldn't save Himself."

Foye Adedokun

Jesus was mocked by one of the thieves, by religious rulers, and by passers-by (Psalm 22:7; Matthew 27).

- That He would be out of strength, so much so that His tongue would stick to the roof of His mouth. While on the cross, Jesus became dehydrated to the point He cried, "I thirst" (Psalm 22:15; John 19).

- That His garment would be divided, and they would cast lots for it. John, the true witness of the crucifixion saga, recorded that the soldiers divided Jesus' garments into four parts, a part to each soldier (Psalm 22:18; John 19).

Nothing that happened to Him came as a surprise. Before reaching each milestone, He knew what He was up against. I wish I can say the same thing about my journey of faith—to know ahead of time when things would be rough and the road would be bumpy; when the journey may get turbulent and my faith would be shaken; when answers to my prayers would be delayed and for how long that would be; when I'll ask and won't receive, seek and won't find, bang on the door so hard and it just won't open. Sadly, I cannot. God alone possesses the power of Alpha and Omega. He alone knows the end even before the beginning.

As human beings, we're limited to only what He lets us know. If Joseph knew what he would suffer before reaching his destination of greatness, he probably would have asked God to forget it. When relating his dreams to his people, he was happy.

4

But that joy soon turned sour and sorrowful when his brothers, out of incontinent envy, turned against him and sold him into slavery. Think of what he suffered in Egypt before he became second-in-command to Pharaoh. Not one moment in those years aligned with his dream of greatness.

Yet, the Lord was with him every step of the way. The journey was rough, but his faith was tough because he knew that his life had been "predestinated according to the purpose of him who worketh all things after the counsel of his own will" (Ephesians 1:11), and that "God is in the heavens. He does whatever he pleases" (Psalm 115:3).

Our journey of faith, though may be turbulent and bumpy. But with God as the Pilot, our flight to heaven will never crash.

What are the odds against you in your journey of faith? Are you at that point where, instead of things getting better, they seem to be getting worse? Instead of Satan relaxing his test of your faith, it's getting harder and tougher. Well, let me remind you that the darkest hour of the night is the hour before dawn. Don't despair and don't lose hope. Christ's journey to Calvary got worse with every step, from His arrest to His crucifixion. But for your sake and mine, He endured until victorious. No matter how bad things get, you too will emerge victorious if you don't give up.

Calvary ordeal can be a direct consequence of poor choices

Let no man say when he is tempted, "I am tempted by God," for God can't be tempted by evil, and he himself tempts no one. But each one is tempted when he is drawn away by his own lust, and enticed. Then the lust, when it has conceived, bears sin; and the sin, when it is full grown, produces death. Don't be deceived, my beloved brothers.
James 1:13-16, WEB

- Many times he was warned about over-speeding and reckless driving. But he never listened. Then one fateful day, he got in a wreck that, luckily, spared his life but left him paralyzed. And unless there's a divine intervention, he'll spend the rest of his life in a wheelchair.

- Her doctors cautioned her about her heavy smoking. She was asked to stop before her situation got worse. Unfortunately, she did not. Now she's dealing with lung cancer. And the daily aches and pains serve as nagging reminders of her terrible choice.

- His parents begged him to quit hanging out with those street boys. They had better plans for him and didn't want anything to happen to him. But he turned deaf ears to their warning because he wanted to have fun. By the time he realized his mistake, it was too late. Caught in the wrong place, at the wrong time, with the wrong group, he would be spending the best part of his life in jail for a crime that he claimed he wasn't part of.

- Because of his lousy lifestyle, he was never there for his children. Their mother raised them alone. Though they suffered many things, eventually, they all survived and are doing well. The tide has now turned on him. He's miserable because he has no place to go and no one to turn to. His children, who are his only hope, have moved on in life, and he has no clue if he can ever find them, much less ask them for help. Life, as he knows it, has ceased to exist.

• Her friends warned her not to marry that man. Those who knew him told her about his quick temper. But she took it the wrong way, thinking they were just jealous that she was getting married to a rich man. Not long after the marriage, she became the rich man's punching bag and the laughingstock of her friends. Now miserable, lonely, and suffering, she wished she had heeded the warnings.

• They were busy doing the kingdom work and had little or no time for the children the owner of the kingdom entrusted into their care. One day, the children were arrested with a gang of cultists and charged with murder. Though they've realized their parental negligence, but it's already too late. The time they're supposed to spend doing the kingdom work is now spent visiting their children in jail.

The above instances are all arbitrary examples to prove that a person can bring crisis upon himself (herself). When the prodigal son left home, he did so of his own accord. Nobody pushed him out of the house. Regrettably, he ran out of resources and was reduced to nothing. He would have gladly eaten the pigs' food, but wasn't allowed. There's no doubt that sometimes, our sufferings are direct consequences of our poor choices. And it will be logical to say that the two thieves were their own worst enemies. It was their awful lifestyle that led them to Golgotha.

Whenever I'm having problems, the first thing I do is search my heart, to see if there's any likelihood that I'm directly responsible for my predicament. Once I give myself a clear check, it makes it easier to tender my case before God, and do so with a clear conscience. I'm not insinuating that you're to blame for what you're passing through right now. But it's not impossible. The Psalmist says, "Search me, O God, and know my heart: try me, and know my thoughts: And see if there be any wicked way in me, and lead me in the way everlasting" (Psalm 139:23-24).

When going through any form of affliction, it's good for believers to first do some soul-searching. That's like clearing the throat before singing because you don't want anything to mess with the melodious flow of your song. Once we know we're in good standing before Him, then we can rest assured that, no matter how bad the problem gets, everything's *gonna* be okay. And if there's any feeling of guilt, the well of God's mercy never runs dry. All He wants from us is to admit our mistakes and ask for forgiveness. He will forgive.

Calvary can happen to a righteous person

In the previous topic, I explained how, by our own poor choices and disobedience, we can push ourselves to Calvary. Here, I like to point out that Calvary crisis can happen to a good and upright person. And none other than our Lord proves that more than anybody. After all, what evil did Jesus commit to deserve Calvary? NONE. Even Pilate found no fault in Him.

Then said Pilate to the chief priests and to the people, I find no fault in this man.
Luke 23:4

And Pilate, when he had called together the chief priests and the rulers and the people, Said unto them, Ye have brought this man unto me, as one that perverteth the people: and, behold, I, having examined him before you, have found no fault in this man touching those things whereof ye accuse him.
Luke 23:13-14

Pilate saith unto him, What is truth? And when he had said this, he went out again unto the Jews, and saith unto them, I find in him no fault at all.
John 18:38

Pilate therefore went forth again, and saith unto them, Behold, I bring him forth to you, that ye may know that I find no fault in him.
John 19:4

When the chief priests therefore and officers saw him, they cried out, saying, Crucify him, crucify him. Pilate saith unto them, Take ye him, and crucify him: for I find no fault in him.
John 19:6

The peace-disturbing question is, if Pilate found no fault in Him, why did he release Him to them? Well, I believe we all know that Jesus suffered because of sinners, and not because of any wrongdoings or guilty charges that anyone successfully brought against Him. And the same can be said of others in the Bible who went through extremely tough times, though accounted as upright and righteous before God. None of them did any evil to deserve the hardship they suffered. But at the end of their stories, they all emerged victorious.

You don't know why you're suffering. You're wondering maybe it's because of a sin that you or someone in your family committed. Please relax. Not all suffering is caused by sin.

And as Jesus passed by, he saw a man which was blind from his birth. And his disciples asked him, saying, Master, who did sin, this man, or his parents, that he was born blind? Jesus answered, Neither hath this man sinned, nor his parents: but that the works of God should be made manifest in him.
John 9:1-3

Sometimes, God permits things to happen so He can glorify Himself in our lives. Just know that no matter how long it lasts, you shall be victorious, in Jesus' Name.

Someone else may be the cause of another person's crisis

As mentioned earlier, suffering and affliction can be direct consequences of poor choices. Sometimes, God allows them either to test our faith or glorify Himself in our lives. But do you know that a person's suffering can be a direct result of someone else's sins or mistakes? There are innocent people living in nightmares that were brought upon them by the actions of others. It would be better if they know the party or parties responsible for their calamities. But many have no clue.

First, think of Jesus on the cross. Unlike the two thieves, He was on the cross for no offense. So why did He have to suffer? It was my sins, your sins, and the sins of mankind that sent Him there. You say yeah, but that was a deliberate choice. Okay, I agree. So let's consider this.

Now the word of the Lord came unto Jonah the son of Amittai, saying, Arise, go to Nineveh, that great city, and cry against it; for their wickedness is come up before me. But Jonah rose up to flee unto Tarshish from the presence of the Lord, and went down to Joppa; and he found a ship going to Tarshish: so he paid the fare thereof, and went down into it, to go with them unto Tarshish from the presence of the Lord. But the Lord sent out a great wind into the sea, and there was a mighty tempest in the sea, so that the ship was like to be broken. Then the mariners were afraid, and cried every man unto his god, and cast forth the wares that were in the ship into the sea, to lighten it of them. . . . And they said every one to his fellow, Come, and let us cast lots, that we may know for

11

whose cause this evil is upon us. So they cast lots, and the lot fell upon Jonah.. . . Wherefore they cried unto the Lord, and said, We beseech thee, O Lord, we beseech thee, let us not perish for this man's life, and lay not upon us innocent blood: for thou, O Lord, hast done as it pleased thee. So they took up Jonah, and cast him forth into the sea: and the sea ceased from her raging.
Jonah 1:1-15 (Emphasis mine)

Those mariners were not there when God asked Jonah to go to Nineveh. They were just going about their normal duties when Jonah brought that evil upon them. Had they not cried unto God in time, they would have perished in the sea because of Jonah's disobedience. *But what's the big deal? The whole thing lasted at most few hours.* You're right. In that case, let's consider one that spanned over four centuries. I'm talking about a whole nation of God's chosen people—the Israelites—who became sojourners in Egypt and suffered immensely for over four hundred years.

Now the sojourning of the children of Israel, who dwelt in Egypt, was four hundred and thirty years.
Exodus 12:40

Those were years of bondage, agony, pain, rejection, hard labor, cruelty, sorrow, suffering, affliction, suppression, oppression, frustration, humiliation, degradation, and deprivation of any human rights, all brought upon them by the sins of some folks in their generation four centuries back.

After selling Joseph into slavery, his brothers thought they

12

had successfully put a period on his life. Fortunately, Joseph made it through years of suffering to become a prime minister in Egypt. Then a famine arose in Israel and the brothers, in search of food, travelled to Egypt, the only nation in the entire land where food was available and in abundance. As fate would have it, no one could purchase food without Joseph's approval. That was where the rubber met the road.

When Joseph saw his brothers, he recognized them, but they didn't recognize him. After a few back-and-forth tricks and treats, he revealed his identity to them. And one can only imagine how bewildered they must have been when they saw the handsome and breathing ghost of their brother, whom they probably thought would have died. With Pharaoh's consent, Joseph relocated the entire brood (seventy people, including aged father, Jacob) from Israel to Egypt. There they lived and thrived, procreating greatly and multiplying immensely. In due course, that generation passed, and so did the familiar Pharaoh.

With the advent of a new Pharaoh, who didn't know Joseph, emerged new but extremely harsh living conditions imposed upon generations of innocent people, who also did not know Joseph and did nothing to deserve the cruelty they suffered (Genesis 37-Exodus 3). And things remained that way until God sent Moses to deliver them out of the land of Egypt.

13

And the LORD said, I have surely seen the affliction of my people which are in Egypt, and have heard their cry by reason of their taskmasters; for I know their sorrows; And I am come down to deliver them out of the hand of the Egyptians, and to bring them up out of that land unto a good land and a large, unto a land flowing with milk and honey; unto the place of the Canaanites, and the Hittites, and the Amorites, and the Perizzites, and the Hivites, and the Jebusites. Now therefore, behold, the cry of the children of Israel is come unto me: and I have also seen the oppression wherewith the Egyptians oppress them. Come now therefore, and I will send thee unto Pharaoh, that thou mayest bring forth my people the children of Israel out of Egypt.
Exodus 3:7-10

Many of them were born into the suffering, lived through the suffering, and died in the suffering, without ever knowing what they did to be treated that way. And to think that the people responsible for their suffering didn't even suffer. In fact, they enjoyed life in abundance at a time of great famine, passing the consequences of their evil acts to their progeny. Speaking of the innocent suffering the punishment meant for the guilty, just like Christ did for me, except He knew why and what He would suffer.

There are times the responsible party's action is deliberate. Other times, it's pure mistake. But whichever way it happens, it hurts to be the unfortunate victim of somebody's actions.

For years, you have been in that condition due to no fault of yours. No doubt that will be painful. Maybe you know the one responsible for it, maybe you don't. Perhaps it was deliberate or it was a mistake. Nonetheless, you wake up every day and wish it was a dream. Your frustration is great and you have no clue what to do. I know what you can do. You can cry to God, just like the children of Israel cried out and God heard their cry.

The righteous cry, and the Lord heareth, and delivereth them out of all their troubles.
Psalm 34:17

Then they cry unto the Lord in their trouble, and he saveth them out of their distresses. He sent his word, and healed them, and delivered them from their destructions.
Psalm 107:19-20

In my distress I cried unto the Lord, and he heard me.
Psalm 120:1

God hears our cries. Cry unto Him and don't stop until He rescues you from that bondage, until He delivers you from that affliction, until He helps you out of that predicament. And no matter what, always remember that God is by your side, to strengthen you when you're weak, to encourage you when you're discouraged, and to lift you up when you're down.

Foye Adedokun

Calvary: Your story, His glory

Whether we're to blame or someone else is to blame for our affliction, the fact remains that Satan is the cause of evil and the one behind any suffering in life. That's why the Bible calls him our adversary.

Be sober, be vigilant; because your adversary the devil, as a roaring lion, walketh about, seeking whom he may devour.
1 Peter 5:8

But as long as we never lose faith, God will turn our story around for His glory.

For almost twenty years that Joseph was away from his folks, the Lord never left him, though life was rough for him. In fact, each time he got out of one ordeal, he got into a harder one. But the end of his story brought glory to the Lord, which was why he was able to forgive his brothers. When he finally revealed his identity to them, he said, "But as for you, ye thought evil against me; but God meant it unto good, to bring to pass, as it is this day, to save much people alive" (Genesis 50:20).

By the time he became prime minister in Egypt, his years of servitude were all worth it. The experience was terrible, but the end was terrific.

The jaw-dropping faith of the Hebrew men—Shadrach, Meshach, and Abednego—should be coveted by anyone who believes in God. It was an amazing faith. But even more amazing

16

than their unyielding faith was the glorious outcome of their story. As a Christian, every Bible miracle puts me in awe of the wonder-working power of God. But to be honest, some of those miracles that involved deliverance—like that of Shadrach, Meshach, and Abednego—make me pray to God to please not test my faith beyond my ability.

If I found myself in their situation, would my faith have passed that rigorous fiery test or would I have caved in for fear? For the sake of my sanity, I'll dismiss those thoughts as mere imaginations of my unfounded apprehension.

Their deliverance from fire is a sure proof of how God can turn our most-chilling Calvary ordeal around for His glory, one that generations after us will read or hear, and stand flabbergasted by the power of faith in the God that never fails.

From their response when Nebuchadnezzar threatened them to bow to his gods, they didn't know how the crisis would end.

Shadrach, Meshach, and Abednego, answered and said to the king, O Nebuchadnezzar, we are not careful to answer thee in this matter. If it be so, our God whom we serve is able to deliver us from the burning fiery furnace, and he will deliver us out of thine hand, O king. But if not, be it known unto thee, O king, that we will not serve thy gods, nor worship the golden image which thou hast set up.
Daniel 3:16-18

Foye Adedokun

It was a "deny God or die" moment. But they were not fazed by fear of fire. And God did not fail them either. In no time, and to the amazement of Nebuchadnezzar, God's Son joined them in the fire and even walked with them, a scene that not only led to Nebuchadnezzar's salvation, but also the promotion of Shadrach, Meshach, and Abednego (Daniel 3:24-30).

I pray that at the end of your trial, the glory of God will be manifested and the shout of Halleluyah shall ring loud and clear in your enemy's ears, in Jesus' Name.

2

Be of Good Cheer

*These things I have spoken unto you, that in me ye might have
peace. In the world ye shall have tribulation: but be of good cheer;
I have overcome the world.*
John 16:33

Trials and tribulations are part of life, a fact made more
realistic by the words of our Savior to His disciples in the
above verse. But knowing that Christ already overcame
on our behalf should make us rest easy, no matter what the
problem is. Except one thing—that's easier said than done. The
man wearing the shoe is the person who can tell where and how
much it hurts.

Some people have been through staggering tragedies, and
there are no words to adequately describe their pain. Some are
going through pains right now—psychological, physical, emotional,
mental, material, and even, spiritual. For some, it's not just one of
those, but some or all of them combined.

Think of Job, a man whose righteousness was attested to by
God (Job 1:2; 2:3). Some people think that if God so vouched for

him, why didn't He prevent Satan from attacking him? And how about Christ, a Man who did good His entire life, only to be murdered by the people He spent His life serving? It's one of those questions to which we'll never get any answers until we see Him in heaven.

But for now, let's address some of the things that will, may, and should happen before, during, and after any Calvary crisis.

What will happen during Calvary crisis

Confusion

As Christ was pushed and dragged to Golgotha, the crowd that followed Him was split between those who wanted Him crucified and those who wanted Him released. And on Calvary, the crescendo of His suffering, some couldn't believe their eyes. "He saved others; himself he cannot save" (Matthew 27:42), they said. But perhaps the most confused person in the crowd would be Mary, His mother. I bet she was as confused as I would be if I were in her shoes. *Am I dreaming? How could this happen to my son? I must be losing my mind. Somebody help me.* Sounds familiar?

A tough time causes confusion, especially when there's no reason to justify the pain and suffering. It's hard to imagine how confused a righteous man like Abraham would be when God asked him to go and sacrifice Isaac, the promised son he waited a quarter of a century to have at hundred years old. How could God give him a child so late and then ask him to go and sacrifice the child? That completely contradicted God's promise to establish His covenant with Isaac, "and with his seed after him" (Genesis 17:19).

Think of the days, the hours, and the minute-by-minute countdown to the day, in absolute confusion *cum* emotional torture. I doubt if he blinked through the night or if he told Sarah about it. What thoughts would be going through his mind when he put the

21

firewood on Isaac and traveled three agonizing days to Moriah (Genesis 22), where he would literally slaughter his own son? And to compound his problem, God didn't stop him one-third of the way there, halfway there, three-quarter way there. Nope. He waited until Abraham reached Moriah and placed Isaac on the altar of sacrifice, the height of his crisis, before He divinely stepped in.

Calvary can get tough to the point we cry, "My God, my God, why hast thou forsaken me?" It's one of those moments when it's hard to distinguish between imaginations and realities. Those moments when God's still small voice becomes totally inaudible, moments when feelings can easily override even the strongest faith, moments when overwhelming sorrow makes us feel abandoned and forsaken by the God we love so much and serve so faithfully, moments when we're clueless on how or what to pray, moments when our only consolation is that God understands how we feel, even though we don't. If you ever get to that stage and feel that way, just hand it over to the Holy Spirit and watch Him turn your confusion into a testimony.

Frustration

I was on the phone with a friend who's going through real trying times. Though we were on the phone, yet, I sensed the deep frustration in my friend's voice. And if it were possible, I would have jumped through the phone, just to share a hug.

A difficult season can be frustrating for many reasons. One, you're in that situation and don't know why. Two, you know why but don't know what to do about it. Three, you know what to do about it but lack the means or ability to make it happen. Four, your problem was caused by someone else, who has since moved on with life. And here you are, struggling to stay alive and wishing it takes less than sixty minutes for an hour to tick by. For you, life has become stagnant. That can be frustrating, exasperating, and downright, inundating.

As a single mother of five, it can be frustrating when you can't provide your children's needs due to financial constraints. That used to be my mother. Poverty? It was worse than that. We lived in penury and fed from hand to mouth. On more occasions than I can recollect, my mother wept out of frustration. Though she loved God, served God, and lived a prayerful life, that didn't change our condition. Now looking back over those years, I realize that God was with us every step of the way. We never had leftovers. But He provided what we needed for each day. One by one, the burden became lighter as the older ones graduated, started working, and started helping. That was part of God's answer to my mother's prayers.

As a man, husband, and father, it can be frustrating losing everything you've worked for in one day. Picture Job's frustration as he received one horrible news after the other, including the tragic death of his ten children. Like the walls of Jericho, his entire world came tumbling down hours or minutes apart. People blame the wife for speaking like someone who had lost her faith in God. Well, to such people, especially mothers, consider yourself in her situation. That woman spoke out of frustration because it can be frustrating when you have no clue why you keep suffering one horrible calamity after another.

- It can be frustrating waiting a quarter of a century to have a child (Genesis 22).

- It can be frustrating to suffer and be imprisoned for years for an offense you didn't commit (Genesis 39).

- It can be frustrating spending years to lead some ingrates through the wilderness, only to miss entering the Promised Land with them because they pushed you till you lost your temper (Numbers 20).

- It can be frustrating for a senior wife to endure years of ridicule from a younger wife, just because she had children and her senior was barren (1 Samuel 1).

- It can be frustrating spending years healing the sick and raising the dead, only to be nailed to the cross like a criminal, though no crimes committed (Matthew 27).

- It can be frustrating missing a healing opportunity for thirty-eight years because no one cared to help (John 5).

At some point in David's life, he was frustrated to an unbearable level where he asked God, "How long?" over and over and over again.

But thou, O LORD, **how long** (Ps. 6:3)?

How long wilt thou forget me, O LORD? for ever? **how long** wilt thou hide thy face from me? **How long** shall I take counsel in my soul, having sorrow in my heart daily? **how long** shall mine enemy be exalted over me (Psalm 13:1-2)?

Lord, **how long** wilt thou look on (Psalm 35:17)?

O God, **how long** shall the adversary reproach (Psalm 74:10)?

How long, LORD? wilt thou be angry for ever (Psalm 79:5)?

How long will ye judge unjustly, and accept the persons of the wicked (Psalm 82:2)?

How long, LORD? wilt thou hide thyself for ever (Psalm 89:46)? LORD, **how long** shall the wicked, **how long** shall the wicked triumph? **How long** shall they utter and speak hard things (Psalm 94:3-4)? (All emphases mine.)

David wasn't asking "how long?" because he had lost faith in God, but because he grew weary of waiting on God to manifest His power. Frustration will make the strongest believer to question God. It will break the heart and crush the spirit because when hope is deferred, the heart becomes sick (Proverbs 13:12).

The good news is, though our afflictions may be many, but the Lord will deliver us "out of them all" (Psalm 34:19). We know when we cry to Him, He hears. When we petition His throne, He listens. And even when our moments of frustration seem to get the best of us, He understands.

Pain

Be prepared for pain when going through crisis. Though pain varies with individuals, but pain is pain. Like I mentioned earlier, for some, it may be physical. And for others, it may be emotional, psychological, or mental. Christ suffered pain before, and, on Calvary; and so did Mary, His mother. Christ's pain on the cross was all inclusive—physical, emotional, psychological, and all. Mary didn't suffer the physical pain of nails. But she suffered enormous mental and psychological pain of watching her Son go through all the torture. She probably never got over the trauma till the day she died.

Anyone going through tough season will experience some form of pain. And because of varying individual tolerance levels, the way one person handles it will be different from the way another person does.

Some believers claim that God uses pain to get our attention. Well, I've been a Christian for years and my attention has never drifted away from God and His Son, Jesus Christ. So why do I still have pain? I'm sure it's not because I took my focus off Him. But through my pain, I'm humbled into total and complete dependence on Him. I'm reminded that, without Him, I am nothing. And by the time I come out of whatever I'm going through, my faith in Him is stronger.

Whatever you're going through, please don't despair. That pain is but for a season and it will definitely pass at God's own appointed time. And if it doesn't end here, eternity will bring a permanent end to it.

Foye Adedokun

What may happen during Calvary crisis

Condemnation

Not every form of condemnation is wrong. If a person commits an offense, he (she) will be condemned in a court of law, and will be dealt some form of punishment as deemed right and lawful by a Judge. As a Christian, if I do something wrong, I feel condemned in my heart as the Holy Spirit convicts me of my wrongdoing. That's perfectly normal.

But the time when someone is going through a rough season is no time for condemnation. Unfortunately, some people see it as a good time to toot their horn of perfection. They're possessed with a judgmental spirit, a holier-than-thou attitude, a purported mega-sized spiritual knowledge, and a bloated religious importance that makes them think they're better than others.

Read the accusations that Job's friends threw at him during his trials.

God killed Job's children because of their disobedience (Job 8:4).

Job took pledges from his brother for nothing (Job 22:6).

Job stripped people of their clothing (Job 22:6).

Job did not give water to the weary (Job 22:7).

Job did not give bread to the hungry (Job 22:7).

Job sent widows away empty-handed (Job 22:9).

Job broke the arms of the fatherless (Job 22:9).

28

Those were some terrible, horrible, miserable friends. That man was hurting already, having tragically lost everything he possessed in one day, followed by an attack on his health. And to utter such condemning statements was to add salt to his injury. Imagine that happening to someone who doesn't have enough faith to bear the criticism, someone whose faith is already dwindling, jerking back and forth like he (she) is about to give up. At such moment, the last thing that individual needs is condemnation.

Jesus experienced the same thing while hanging on the cross. To some unlearned minds, the reason He didn't come down from the cross was because He lacked the power to do so. All the miracles He performed before then were no longer relevant. His hanging on the cross had voided any initial trust or faith they had in Him.

If you experience condemnation from people during your Calvary ordeal, just turn deaf ears and let them rant on. Let the dogs bark, for it's their nature to do so. You stay strong in the Lord, and soon, you will be singing the songs of victory.

Disappointment

Disappointment happens every day. Failed examinations, dwindling health, unanswered prayers, abusive spouse, unjustified employment termination, betrayal, demotion in place of promotion, unsuccessful job interviews, missed opportunities, *et cetera.* And none of them is easy to cope with. But worse than any of those is

29

disappointment from the ones we trust the most—a father who could care less about his kids; a mother who would rather do drugs than take care of her children; a spouse who shuns the vow to love and cherish, and instead treats his (her) spouse like a piece of trash; children who soon forget everything the parents went through to get them to where they are.

Disappointment hurts, especially during difficult times. But it's nothing new. Even Jesus experienced disappointment during His difficult moments. Really? Yes, really.

They came to a place which was named Gethsemane. . . . He took with him Peter, James, and John, and began to be greatly troubled and distressed. He said to them, "My soul is exceedingly sorrowful, even to death. Stay here, and watch." He went forward a little, and fell on the ground, and prayed that, if it were possible, the hour might pass away from him. . . . He came and found them sleeping, and said to Peter, "Simon, are you sleeping? Couldn't you watch one hour? . . . Again he went away, and prayed, saying the same words. Again he returned, and found them sleeping, for their eyes were very heavy, and they didn't know what to answer him. He came the third time, and said to them, "Sleep on now, and take your rest. It is enough. The hour has come. Behold, the Son of Man is betrayed into the hands of sinners. Arise, let us be going. Behold, he who betrays me is at hand."
Mark 14:32-42, WEB

At that point in His life, the stress of the journey became extremely overwhelming. And the dread of an impending death weighed down heavily on Him, so much so that His body slipped into *hematidrosis*, a rare medical condition when extreme fear or stress causes the body's tiny blood vessels to burst and normal body sweats turn into bloody sweats.

And being in an agony he prayed more earnestly: and his sweat was as it were great drops of blood falling down to the ground.
Luke 22:44

He thought He could draw some succor from Peter, James, and John, one of whom had vowed his support, even if it meant losing his life (Mark 14:29-31). He needed a shoulder to lean on. Normally, three shoulders should be more than enough. If one failed, the other two would not. If James and John failed, Peter would NEVER fail. He already pledged his unfailing support. But at a time He needed them most, none of them sufficed, not even the solid-as-a-rock Peter. Just an hour of support was all He asked for, but that obviously was too much for them to offer.

Don't be alarmed or offended when your trusted ones are nowhere to be found when you need them the most. Sometimes, their actions are not deliberate. Their spirit may be truly willing to help you, but their flesh is too weak to pull through for you. And even when their actions are deliberate, remember that your cross is your burden and not that of anyone else, no matter how close.

If people offer their support during your crisis, receive it with gratitude. If not, move on with your life, knowing that you

31

have Jesus, the greatest support, helper, and burden bearer, always by your side. It may not seem like He's there, but trust me, He is. And He feels your pain because He went through exact same thing that you're going through.

Doubt

There's no better time for Satan to make a believer doubt God than during trying seasons. So far, life is good and everything is going as planned—financially, materially, spiritually, physically. Without warning, the tides turn and you find yourself seeking help from the people you used to help. Incessant prayers from you and fellow brethren have availed nothing. If anything, things are only getting worse. Good moment for the devil to quickly chip in.

If God truly cares about you, why is He allowing all these? How can He do this to you? Why is He allowing Satan to mess with you? After all, nothing can happen to you unless He permits it.

And since he'll stop at nothing, he sends people to you. They may be your close friends who have suddenly turned into theologians of divine retribution. Like Job's friends, they tell you that God only permits evil to happen to evil people. Before you know it, you're thinking about the things they tell you. Their words keep replaying over and over in your brain. At that moment, you need to apply God's Word to counteract the thoughts before you start believing them.

The worst stage is when you walk out of God's love, and in

the process, lose your salvation because you think God doesn't care anymore. We must "Take heed, brethren, lest there be in any of you an evil heart of unbelief, in departing from the living God" (Hebrews 3:12).

I know suffering can make anyone doubt God's love. It's hard not to doubt God when everything is going contrary to His promises for us. It's hard not to doubt the love of a just and good God, Who boasts of your righteousness but didn't stop Satan from destroying all you have. It's hard not to doubt the faithfulness of His promises when sons of Belial are prospering and progressing, while the faithful tithers and believers struggle to make ends meet. It's hard not to doubt God when the righteous dies young, but the wicked lives long. It's hard to imagine light when surrounded by total darkness.

Based on our knowledge of God and His promises, what we're dealing with completely contradicts what we think should be the case. And yes, that will cast a shadow of doubt on any faith. But that mindset is Satan's ploy to make you stray from the truth. Once you sense the spirit of doubt taking over, it calls for serious prayers. Don't take it lightly because that only leaves a crack in the wall for the enemy to crawl in and destroy you. Even when you think you have a genuine reason to doubt, refuse to doubt God's love for you.

Foye Adedokun

Rejection

Going through a difficult season is hard, and so is rejection from those we think would or should be there for us. I know rejection is painful because I've traveled that road before. It's easy to forget a friend's rejection. But to be rejected by a father is sickening and devastating. My father never granted me, or any of my siblings, the acceptance a child craves from a parent—a loving parent. And the truth be told, the pain never fully goes away. But with age and with God, it gets easier to cope with.

While going through your Calvary journey, you may suffer rejection from those closest or dearest to you. Your trusted folks suddenly distance themselves from you. They were very much around when the going was good. They visited you uninvited. You had so much merrymaking that people on your street thought it was always Christmas in your house.

Now there's barely enough, and what used to be leftovers are now the main meals. Soon, you went from lender to borrower. The friends you helped on numerous occasions are all gone. They always told you that if you ever needed help, you could count on them. Those turned out to be empty barrel, all-bark-and-no-bite promises. You crossed the ocean for them, but they can't cross the puddle for you. Like the friends of the prodigal son, they loved you in prosperity and left you in adversity.

Maybe it's bad health. The branch falls, the bird flies off.

The spouse who loved you so much is nowhere to be found. Your employer fires you because you can no longer perform your duties as expected. Left without income, your bad health is about to get worse. One rejection after another. But nothing new, really. Even Christ suffered rejection from trusted disciples and followers. One moment, He was hailed as the Christ. Next moment, He was nailed as a criminal.

He is despised and rejected of men; a man of sorrows, and acquainted with grief: and we hid as it were our faces from him; he was despised, and we esteemed him not.
Isaiah 53:3

And they all forsook him, and fled.
Mark 14:50

If it happened to Jesus, I guess it can happen to anybody. Don't let it bother you because "we know that all things work together for good to them that love God, to them who are the called according to his purpose" (Romans 8:28).

When brown leaves fall off a tree in Autumn, the tree looks bare, not too pleasant to behold. But that process is necessary to get the tree ready for a new look, when it'll spring back to life with fresh green leaves. When folks reject you during your tough season, consider it a weeding and shedding process of the bad elements in your life. At the end, your life will be much better without them.

35

Foye Adedokun

Separation

As Jesus hung on the cross, one of the two thieves saw it as a good moment to mock Him. The other thief rebuked him. But he didn't stop at rebuking. He quickly distanced himself from him by asking Jesus to remember him in His Kingdom (Luke 23:39-43). He will spend eternity in heaven while his unrepentant comrade will spend eternity in hell fire. It doesn't get any farther apart than that.

Do you feel something unspiritual about someone you call a friend? Do you feel stuck in a bad relationship? Do you have an undue attraction to someone with negative values? Do you feel the need to give Jesus a chance in your life, but you don't want to lose your friend? Perhaps it's time for you to reevaluate your priorities. Of what use to you is someone who is not adding any value to your life? To soar high like an eagle, refrain from the company of chickens. Separate yourself from any relationship that can hinder your progress or prayer for breakthrough.

Even if a person has been a friend forever, if such won't give serious consideration to salvation, you may need to distance yourself from him (her) for the sake of your eternity. Remember that two cannot walk together unless they agree (Amos 3:3). And it is a known fact that the company you keep will either make you or break you, either for good or bad.

To flourish like the palm tree and grow like a cedar in

Lebanon, you must avoid the flourishing workers of iniquity and the wicked who spring like the grass. Otherwise, you will suffer the same everlasting destruction that shall come upon them (Psalm 92). Choose your friends wisely. If it becomes necessary for you to separate yourself from that person, don't hesitate to do exactly that.

What to do during Calvary crisis

Be realistic

For verily I say unto you, That whosoever shall say unto this mountain, Be thou removed, and be thou cast into the sea; and shall not doubt in his heart, but shall believe that those things which he saith shall come to pass; he shall have whatsoever he saith.
Mark 11:23

I have a problem and I know that I have a problem. Does having faith and staying positive interpret as living in denial of the problem? I don't know what other believers think, but I don't think so. Of what use is my faith during trials, when I don't even admit that I have trials? Why would I exercise faith asking God to end my suffering if I'm not suffering?

Commanding a non-existent mountain to move is madness, not faith. The Bible doesn't say we should act like the problem is not real. There's not one verse in the Bible where the reality of Christ's sufferings before Calvary and on Calvary were denied. Every account about Calvary is real, including the pain and agony of crucifixion, which made Him cry to His Father.

As a sufferer of rheumatoid arthritis, I know how H.A.R.D pain feels. It's **h**orrible, **a**wful, **r**uthless, **d**ebilitating. Sometimes, I wish I can jump out of my body, just to get some relief. Some days are harder than others, and the only thing I want to do is question

God. I know the pain is real because I feel it. But instead of faking or pretending, I ask God to cease or ease my pain.

Trials and tests of faith are part of life, no escape. Godly people in the Bible had trials and they maintained great faith until they overcame. But they didn't deny the reality of their problems.

- Abraham did not deny the reality of his childlessness or that of Sarah's dead womb (Genesis 15:2-3).

- Moses and the Israelites did not deny the reality of the Red Sea before them, and the Egyptian army behind them (Exodus 14:13-14).

- When the Israelites encountered bitter waters at Marah, they knew that meant no water to drink. As usual, they turned their frustration on Moses (Exodus 15:23-25).

- In Jericho, they encountered the virtually impenetrable walls of Jericho, adding to the number of obstacles they had to overcome before reaching the Promised Land. Facing the reality of it was why they marched around the city for seven days before the walls came tumbling down (Joshua 6).

- Hannah wept before the Lord because she was barren, and she did not deny it (1 Samuel 1:9-11).

- Naaman traveled to see Elisha in Samaria to seek healing from leprosy. Obviously, he didn't deny it (2 Kings 5).

- Shadrach, Meshach, and Abednego never acted like the fire wasn't real (Daniel 3:17).

- When Daniel was to be tossed into the lions' den, believe me he knew where he was going—inside a real den with real lions (Daniel 6).

- The leper did not deny the reality of his leprosy (Matthew 8:2).

- The woman with twelve years issue of blood did not deny the reality of it (Matthew 9:20-22).

- The deaf and dumb agreed to be brought to Jesus because he knew he needed healing (Mark 7:31-36).

- When Jesus asked blind Bartimaeus, "What do you want me to do for you?" he replied, "Rabbi, I want to see." He never denied the reality of his blindness (Mark 10:46-52).

- Why do you think Jairus, the Ruler, came running to Jesus? Because his daughter was sick, which later resulted in death before Jesus raised her back to life (Luke 8:41-42, 49-56).

- And for the man born blind, the Pharisees told him it was impossible for Jesus to restore his sight because Jesus was a sinner. But he minced no words setting them straight.

Whether he be a sinner or no, I know not: one thing I know, that, whereas I was blind, now I see.
John 9:25

All these and many more prove that those people never denied their problems. What Calvary hill are you climbing right now? Barrenness, spiritual affliction, joblessness, health problems, financial turbulence, marital problems, wayward children? I know the cross is heavy and the mountain is steep. But what good would it do denying it? Shun the pretense and face reality. That doesn't mean you lack the power of positive thinking. It just means you understand what you're up against and you're ready to deal with it. Then by a prayer of faith, command the mountain to move. Don't negotiate with it to move. Don't persuade it to move. Don't plead with it to move. Without hesitation, command it to move.

Repent

Repenting of past sins is the first step to salvation. No sinner can be saved without first repenting of his (her) sins. *But the thief on the cross didn't repent of his sins.* Oh yes, he did.

And one of the malefactors which were hanged railed on him, saying, If thou be Christ, save thyself and us. But the other answering rebuked him, saying, Dost not thou fear God, seeing thou art in the same condemnation? And we indeed justly; for we receive the due reward of our deeds: but this man hath done nothing amiss. And he said unto Jesus, Lord, remember me when thou comest into thy kingdom.
Luke 23:39-42

Repentance is a realization of wrongdoing, an admission of guilt, and a desire to forsake the bad life for a better life. And that was exactly what he did. His admission of guilt was embedded in his rebuke of the other thief. That statement has an undertone

41

of godly sorrow, which "produces repentance to salvation" (2 Corinthians 7:10, WEB). He was sorrowful for his past actions that led to his present predicament. Having done that, the way was cleared for him to ask the Savior to remember him in His kingdom.

Behold, the Lord's hand is not shortened, that it cannot save; neither his ear heavy, that it cannot hear: But your iniquities have separated between you and your God, and your sins have hid his face from you, that he will not hear.
Isaiah 59:1-2

Had he not repented, Christ wouldn't have granted his wish because God doesn't hear the prayers of a sinner (John 9:31). If you're yet to be saved, or saved but fell back into sin, you must first renounce your sins, repent of them, and determine to live a godly life, so God can hear your prayers and, either deliver you from your affliction or give you the grace to get through it.

We serve a righteous and loving God. But nothing repels Him like the odor of sin. If we want to enjoy His presence, we must part with sin. That doesn't mean that repenting of sins gives automatic immunity from physical adversity. It may remove or reduce it, and it may not. After receiving the promise of eternity, the thief still suffered the pain and agony of crucifixion till he died. But he made heaven where he'll never know pain again.

After his conversion, Paul got radical for the gospel, ready to go any length for the works of the kingdom he opposed for years.

He was so anointed that he commanded a lame man to stand on his feet, and the man "leaped and walked" (Acts 14:8-10). Yet, his own physical body, which he needed to go from place to place, suffered an ailment from which he was never healed (2 Corinthians 12:7-10).

When the paralytic was brought to Jesus by four men, Jesus said to him, "Son, be of good cheer; **thy sins** be forgiven thee" (Matthew 9:2, emphasis mine). Jesus addressed his sins before his sickness because anyone who is forgiven and refrains from sinning will make heaven, regardless of physical challenges or handicap. But physical deliverance without deliverance from sins avails nothing. A forgiven paralytic will enter heaven, no doubt. But a sinful paralytic will go to hell, call it double trouble. Repent so you can be forgiven.

Restitute (See page 270 for more on restitution.)

Repentance is vital to salvation. But it must be followed up with proper restitution, when possible. Restitution is returning to the owner, something that doesn't belong to you, but is deliberately or mistakenly taken by you, or, deliberately or mistakenly put in your possession. If you know or have the means to make things right, obligation compels you to do something about it. To claim you have repented without restitution is to profess righteousness while sin lies still at your door.

God wants you to turn from your wicked ways. But He also wants you to restore whatever you have robbed (Ezekiel 33:14-15). None illustrates this better than Zacchaeus in the Bible.

And Jesus entered and passed through Jericho. And, behold, there was a man named Zacchaeus, which was the chief among the publicans, and he was rich. And he sought to see Jesus who he was; and could not for the press, because he was little of stature. And he ran before, and climbed up into a sycomore tree to see him: for he was to pass that way. And when Jesus came to the place, he looked up, and saw him, and said unto him, Zacchaeus, make haste, and come down; for to day I must abide at thy house. And he made haste, and came down, and received him joyfully. And when they saw it, they all murmured, saying, That he was gone to be guest with a man that is a sinner. And Zacchaeus stood, and said unto the Lord: Behold, Lord, the half of my goods I give to the poor; and if I have taken any thing from any man by false accusation, I restore him fourfold. And Jesus said unto him, This day is salvation come to this house, forsomuch as he also is a son of Abraham.
Luke 19:1-9

By virtue of their vocation, tax collectors are notorious and hardly on good terms with people. And Zacchaeus happened to be one such individual, who enriched himself by making people pay more than required by law. But when he encountered Jesus, he restored fourfold of everything he falsely took from others.

Restitution is not only important for personal reasons. But for the sake of those directly or remotely connected to us, we need to get rid of accursed things in our possession to avoid the evil aftermaths on us and them, as the case was with Achan.

Achan took forbidden items and stole precious elements belonging to the Lord's house. Had he returned those things within the ample chance that he had to restitute, he would have escaped the fiery judgment. But he failed to do that and brought a terrible evil, not just upon himself, but his entire family who knew nothing about his bizarre behavior (Joshua 7). Don't let that be said of you.

Restitution can be hindered by a couple of factors.

One, a person genuinely wants to restitute but cannot for lack of time. If the repentant thief lived longer than he did after his salvation, he probably would have returned any stolen items still in his possession, or paid the monetary value to the owners. But time failed him to do that.

Two, there's a sincere desire to restitute, but it's beyond one's ability—like a large sum of money that had been spent and forgotten. It's no longer an issue of not wanting to return the money, but an inability to come up with the huge amount. If it's possible to find the owner, a direct confession must be made to secure forgiveness from the person.

Let me also mention that no restitution is too big or too small to make. There were times I went back to the store to pay the difference between what I was supposed to pay and what I saw on the receipt. It wasn't much, but much enough to me. No years of repentance can save you from hell if you have wrongly amassed things to yourself and you do nothing about it. They're foreign gods that you need to put away as an act of purification (Genesis 35:2-4), so God can grant your petitions.

Do you sense the need to make a restitution? False tax claims for bigger refunds, forged documents, items taken from work, false declarations on any documents, embezzlement, getting paid more than required for work done, selling fake items for the price of original, unpaid borrowed money, or money spent without owner's permission?

If you can't remember, prayerfully ask the Holy Spirit to remind you of any restitution/s you need to make. If you don't know how to go about it, seek counsel from a godly individual. And when it's absolutely impossible, I believe God understands. But do what you need to do, so your prayers are not hindered.

Have faith

There's a mountain standing in your way and you know it. The problem is real and you see it, feel it, and therefore, admit it. But you want it removed. That requires faith. You know that faith is not a denial of a mountain, but a belief that God will help you make the mountain disappear.

I can move a heavy object without help, if it's not too heavy. But there are times I need help because the object is heavier than I can handle. When the latter is the case, I call someone who can help, not someone who cannot. We exercise faith in God because we trust Him to help us deal with a situation that is beyond our human ability.

The woman with the issue of blood did everything humanly possible to be healed of her bleeding, all to no avail. But knowing that the great Healer—Jesus Christ—was in town, she determined that was an opportunity she would not miss.

Faith is an exercise of trust in a higher power to help you accomplish that which you cannot accomplish in your ordinary human strength.

And, behold, a woman, which was diseased with an issue of blood twelve years, came behind him, and touched the hem of his garment: For she said within herself, If I may but touch his garment, I shall be whole. But Jesus turned him about, and when he saw her, he said, Daughter, be of good comfort; thy faith hath made thee whole. And the woman was made whole from that hour.
Matthew 9:20-22

There was only one obstacle standing between her problem and her miracle—getting through the crowd to make the divine touch. Just a touch and her twelve-year crisis would be over. She said, "I shall be whole." Not, *Maybe I will be whole; perhaps I will be whole; let's see if I will be whole.* But, *I shall be whole,* period. And when she did, her misery became history.

My dear brother or sister, don't stop trusting the power of God. He won't ask you to call upon Him in the day of trouble if He's not able to deliver you (Psalm 50:15). Put your faith into action and command that mountain in your life to disappear. From this moment, it shall be a once-upon-a-time ordeal that you will only use to tell others about the power of faith in a mountain-moving God, in Jesus' Name.

Remain prayerful

As Christians, the Bible asks us to "pray without ceasing" (1 Thessalonians 5:17), which can be done anywhere. But I believe prayer should be more intense during afflictions because desperate situation calls for desperate intercession. Victory is neither cheap nor easy. If need be, ask other believers to join you in prayer, like apostle Paul did in his time of desperation.

Now I beseech you, brethren, for the Lord Jesus Christ's sake, and for the love of the Spirit, that ye strive together with me in your prayers to God for me; That I may be delivered from them that do not believe in Judaea; and that my service which I have for Jerusalem may be accepted of the saints.
Romans 15:30-31

Requesting the help of other believers for prayer is a sign of spiritual humility. It can be your church members or a group of fellow believers, far or near. Be open to godly people. After all, you don't gain anything acting proud during affliction. That will only compound your problems. Don't get weary until your prayers are answered. Pray anywhere, everywhere, anytime, and every time. God is Omnipresent, everywhere, every time. Be it in the lions' den or the belly of a fish, on the highest mountain or in the lowest valley, He can hear your voice. Keep praying until victory is won.

Be at peace

I should be in the Guinness book of world records as the worst liar if I said it's easy to be at peace during trying times. I know it's not easy, because nothing drains peace like uncertainty, a constant by-product of a difficult season.

- How can a person be at peace when stuck between the perils of a mighty Red Sea and the pursuit of a monstrous army?
- How can a person be at peace when he's about to be thrown inside a furnace of raging fire?
- How can a person be at peace when he's about to be fed to lions?
- How can a person be at peace when faced with legal troubles that he (she) has nothing to do with?
- How can a person be at peace when he (she) has no idea where the next meal will come from?
- How can a person be at peace when the landlord is already threatening eviction due to unpaid rent?
- How can someone be at peace when there are clear indications that he (she) will soon lose that health battle?

Nothing gets a person aggravated and frustrated like lack of peace. Yet, the Bible wants us to be at peace, no matter what. As passengers trust the pilot during turbulence and through the entire journey, God wants us to trust Him, not just in turbulent times, but throughout our journey of faith.

Thou wilt keep him in perfect peace, whose mind is stayed on thee: because he trusteth in thee.
Isaiah 26:3

That's peace beyond human understanding. People may not understand why you're praising God when you should be freaking out. Some may even think you need help because you're obviously losing your mind. Don't worry. Very soon, God will prove Himself to them through you.

Be patient

The world is full of impatient people. On the road, inside the house, in the store, in the workplace, in the hospital, even inside the church, of all places to be impatient. Where are we going and why so much in a hurry? Because of impatience on the road, many end their lives and those of innocent citizens. Couples impatiently walk out of their marriages. Students fail their tests because it's a waste of time trying to correct possible errors. Sadly, that's the same attitude some believers have during trials and tough seasons.

Most Christians know what a waiting period means. It's the time between expectation and actualization, the time we spend waiting for requests to morph into realities. For some, it is short. For others, it takes forever between waiting and receiving. Every positive thinking has been thought. Every miracle prayer has been prayed. Every promise in the Bible has been claimed, tears have been shed, praises have been sung. And still, no answer, not even a dream. The believer is left asking why, why, oh why? That can be very perplexing. But let's not forget that God is not operating on the same time pattern as man.

For a thousand years in thy sight are but as yesterday when it is past, and as a watch in the night.
Psalm 90:4

But, beloved, be not ignorant of this one thing, that one day is with the Lord as a thousand years, and a thousand years as one day.
2 Peter 3:8

Very true are the words of this stanza from the age enduring hymn—Oh God, Our Help in Ages Past.

A thousand ages in Thy sight
Are like an evening gone;
Short as the watch that ends the night
Before the rising sun (Isaac Watts, 1719).

That Abraham waited twenty-five years to have Isaac only comes down to few minutes by God's timing, not even up to an hour. To God, what we call long waiting is like the same amount of time it takes to blink—so unnoticeably transient. And we still wonder why He's never in a hurry. He's a God of time as in seasons, not time according to our clock or calendar. And by seasons, I don't mean Spring, Summer, Autumn, Winter, wet, or dry season. Every phase of our life—birth, good times, bad times, and death—is a season.

To every thing there is a season, and a time to every purpose under the heaven: A time to be born, and a time to die; a time to plant, and a time to pluck up that which is planted.
Ecclesiastes 3:1-2

The period of barrenness is a season, and so is the period of joblessness, regardless of the duration. The man born blind passed through a season, and so did the man born lame. Hannah endured a season, and so did Ruth. The bent woman's season lasted eighteen years. For the Israelites, their season lasted four hundred and thirty years. But at God's own time, each

Time appointed by God to end our suffering is not contingent on our patience or impatience. He has different reasons for different seasons, and different times for different trials.

season came to an end. Faith requires patience to wait on God in absolute submission and total yieldedness to His will, even when His will is at war with our flesh, the adamic nature.

We can be in a hurry all we want, it won't change a thing.

James says the trying of our faith works patience (James 1:3). Unnecessary hurry will only lead to a spiritual wreck. By the time we realize our erring, the damage is already done and the mistake is too late to correct. Don't be in a hurry. Your perilous times are temporal, not eternal. It's only a season and it won't last forever. Christ's crucifixion didn't last forever, but the glory that followed it will last through all eternity.

We must also be patient with those who may offend us during our trials, either by their words or actions. Many of them act in ignorance and mean no harm. And getting upset won't help the situation. Be patient so you can be victorious. "Wait on the LORD: be of good courage, and he shall strengthen thine heart: wait, I say, on the LORD" (Psalm 27:14).

Be temperate

Temperance is the ability to exercise self-control in any situation, and especially, under the direst circumstances when your flesh really wants to react. Think of that great opportunity that Joseph had to take revenge on his brothers when they came to Egypt to buy food. Instead, he controlled his emotions and forgave them (Genesis 50:18-20).

Consider on how many occasions Jesus could have dealt some holy blows to the faces of the religious rulers who seemed to derive pleasure from jabbing insults at Him. It happened through

His entire ministry and continued all the way to Golgotha. They even tortured Him as He hung on the cross. But the Bible says, "Who, when he was reviled, reviled not again; when he suffered, he threatened not" (1 Peter 2:23). He endured it all without striking back.

While going through hard times, temperance will help you in two ways. One, it will restrain you from taking vengeance on those responsible for your problem, if you know them. Two, it will help you look the other way from the holy bullies who will take advantage of your vulnerability to insult you because they think they're better than you.

Some people are so good at making other people miserable and they will seize any opportunity to do that. They're spiritual distractors sent from the pit of hell to make a believer lose focus. If they succeed, you can no longer pray as before because you're still offended by what that person said to you. Or worse, you're angry and ashamed because of the way you reacted, quite unlike a child of God. Now you wish you had said nothing.

I've been in situations where I just couldn't resist reacting, which only added more fuel to the fire. But over the years, I've learned that silence is golden and I don't have to answer my critics. And going by the general belief that life is ten percent what happens to us and ninety percent how we react to it, it means I have very little control over how people treat me, but I have a huge control over how I react to the treatment. So instead of giving that stern-faced, eye-rolling, mouth-running response, I just smile and say nothing. I've done that on more occasions than I can count.

Is it easy? NO!!! But trust me, it works wonders. Before long, God Himself deals with my accuser. Case settled. If you lack self-control, ask God to give it to you.

Maintain your focus

Almost every State in America has banned the use of cell phones while driving. It's not because of cell phones, but the distractions caused when using them behind the wheel. People run onto railroads without noticing the signal lights of an approaching train. By the time they look up, it's too late. Innocent lives are lost every day because drivers take their eyes off the road to use the phone. They think it only takes few seconds to send a quick text message. But they forget that's exactly how long it takes for accidents to happen.

Likewise in our spiritual journey, distractions are sure to come, especially during trying times because we're more prone to losing focus when life gets stormy.

How will my family survive the month? What do I do? Where do I go? Should I talk to somebody? What will people think?

While thinking about your problems, your unbeliever work colleague walks over to you. He's also dealing with some issues in his life, and you're the person he trusts to share them with. But the moment you open your mouth to tell him about the unfailing love of God, Satan reminds you of your own problems. He takes your focus off of God's faithfulness, so you can begin to doubt Him and, maybe, quit telling others about Him.

Even when things aren't going well, keep your focus on the Savior. Consider it a light affliction that will only be for a moment.

For which cause we faint not; but though our outward man perish, yet the inward man is renewed day by day. For our light affliction, which is but for a moment, worketh for us a far more exceeding and eternal weight of glory; While we look not at the things which are seen, but at the things which are not seen: for the things which are seen are temporal; but the things which are not seen are eternal.
2 Corinthians 4:16-18

Wherefore seeing we also are compassed about with so great a cloud of witnesses, let us lay aside every weight, and the sin which doth so easily beset us, and let us run with patience the race that is set before us, <u>Looking unto Jesus</u> the author and finisher of our faith; who for the joy that was set before him endured the cross, despising the shame, and is set down at the right hand of the throne of God.
Hebrews 12:1-2 (Emphasis mine)

When Peter attempted to walk on water to Jesus, everything was fine until he took his eyes off the Savior and started looking at the strong wind (Matthew 14:25-30). I believe you don't want to sink into the sea of life. For that not to happen, keep your eyes on the Savior, so you don't lose your balance—body, soul, and spirit. Hold on tight and steadfast, laser-focused on God and God only. And if you're already losing it, do what Peter did. Call on Jesus to save you, and He will.

Maintain a positive attitude

•   As Abraham journeyed to Mount Moriah where he was to sacrifice Isaac, he made two positive declarations.

One, he told the young men travelling with him, "Abide ye here with the ass; and I and the lad will go yonder and worship, and come again to you" (Genesis 22:4-5).
Isaac was the lad. If he was going to sacrifice him, how could both come again?

Two, when Isaac asked, "Where is the lamb for a burnt offering?" Abraham replied, "My son, God will provide himself a lamb for a burnt offering" (Genesis 22:7-8).
God already asked him to go and sacrifice his son, Isaac. He was the lamb. So what other lamb was he expecting God to provide?

See, Abraham walked by faith. His replies were based on the promise he received even before Isaac was born. God already said He would establish His covenant with Isaac, "and with his seed after him" (Genesis 17:19). Abraham knew that if God said it, it would surely come to pass. For Isaac to bear seeds, he had to be alive. Therefore, no need to fret because Isaac would not die.

That's called staying positive when everything is going in the negative direction.

• At the Red Sea, Moses told the Israelites, "Fear ye not, stand still, and see the salvation of the LORD, which he will shew to you to day: for the Egyptians whom ye have seen to day, ye shall see them again no more for ever" (Exodus 14:13).

Did he not see the Red Sea in front of them, and Pharaoh's massive army closing in from behind them?

Yes, he did. But he stayed positive when everything seemed to be going in the negative direction.

• Compared to Goliath, David was nowhere close in height, weight, or arsenal.

A champion out of the camp of the Philistines named Goliath, of Gath, whose height was six cubits and a span went out. He had a helmet of brass on his head, and he wore a coat of mail; and the weight of the coat was five thousand shekels of brass. He had brass shin armor on his legs, and a brass javelin between his shoulders. The staff of his spear was like a weaver's beam; and his spear's head weighed six hundred shekels of iron. His shield bearer went before him.
1 Samuel 17:4-7, WEB

Like that wasn't intimidating enough for a man of David's stature to take off running.

And he took his staff in his hand, and chose him five smooth stones out of the brook, and put them in a shepherd's bag which he had, even in a scrip; and his sling was in his hand: and he drew near to the Philistine. Thou comest to me with a sword, and with a spear, and with a shield: but I come to thee in the name of the LORD of hosts, the God of the armies of Israel, whom thou hast defied. This day will the LORD deliver thee into mine hand; and I will smite thee, and take thine head from thee; and I will give the carcases of the host of the Philistines this day unto the fowls of the air, and to the wild beasts of the earth; that all the earth may know that there is a God in Israel. And all this assembly shall know that the LORD saveth not with sword and spear: for the battle is the LORD's, and he will give you into our hands.
1 Samuel 17:40, 45-47

All that confidence with five smooth stones and a sling? That joker definitely didn't notice the humongous creature standing in front of him.

Make no mistake. David saw Goliath and everything on him. But because he knew that God doesn't save with spear and sword, he maintained a victory attitude even when it appeared like he was about to fight an already concluded lost battle. The Bible says, "The LORD shall fight for you, and ye shall hold your peace" (Exodus 14:14). When you make God the Giant in your battles, He will decapitate every giant in your life and give you unprecedented victory.

• As Shadrach, Meshach, and Abednego were about to be thrown inside fire, they told King Nebuchadnezzar, "If it be so, our God whom we serve is able to deliver us from the burning fiery furnace, and he will deliver us out of thine hand, O king" (Daniel 3:17).

Those three must be blind. They either didn't see the fire or they didn't know its intensity.

Yes, they saw it and they knew its intensity. But they maintained a positive attitude even when the situation clearly looked negative.

Everybody experiences some type of unpleasant situation in life. The saved thief faced an unpleasant situation as he hung on the cross. But so did our Savior. And candidly speaking, it can be difficult to maintain a positive attitude when everything looks negative, when the events don't line up with the Word of God, or when there's no explicable justification for the situation. To those around us, a positive attitude in such a negative atmosphere is subtle insanity. I say that's okay. But don't bring greater evil upon your life with negative utterances.

Death and life are in the power of the tongue.
Proverbs 18:21

For he that will love life, and see good days, let him refrain his tongue from evil, and his lips that they speak no guile.
1 Peter 3:10

The words we speak have immense power on the mind. If a person believes that he (she) will die of a disease, the chances of survival are slim. Considering the pain of crucifixion, the saved thief had every reason to be negative. After all, he would soon die and go to hell. But even in that negative situation he was in, he found a way to bring something positive out of it. He turned to Jesus and asked to be with Him in His kingdom. A thief in Christ's kingdom? That guy got some nerve. Well, nerve is what it takes to stay positive.

When we act negative during tough times, thinking the situation will never get better, Satan feels glorified. It's an indirect way of accepting his verdict upon our lives. We must constantly ask the Holy Spirit to help us control our thoughts, "For out of the abundance of the heart the mouth speaketh" (Matthew 12:34). If you can't control your thoughts, ask God to set a watch before your mouth; and to keep the door of your lips (Psalm 141:3). That should take care of any negative confessions.

Forgive

I wish I can tell you that nobody will hurt your feelings during your trials, but I dare not. Try all you want, someone is going to offend you during hardship. Maybe it's because we're more emotionally unstable under pressure, thus easily offended. Or, maybe people are just hard of feelings for the helpless. Hard to say, really. However, nothing that anyone does to us is a good excuse for unforgiveness. And Christ demonstrated that on the cross when He asked His Father to forgive His killers, even as they nailed Him to the cross.

Why the need to forgive those who offend you in time of difficulty? The reason is so you can be released from bondage. Bitterness is toxic and dangerous to your health. When you harbor resentment, you're the victim and it affects every aspect of your life. Physically, you will look haggard. Emotionally, you will be unstable. Spiritually, your actions won't align with your profession of faith.

If you let the offense of anybody make you turn your back on everybody, the time will come when you'll need the help of somebody, but there will be nobody to help you.

It'll be a different story if the offender knows that he (she) has offended you. But the person is totally unaware of the situation, while you keep boiling over nothing. I know it can be difficult to forgive someone who makes an already bad situation worse with bitter remarks and insinuations. But you don't gain anything by refusing to forgive them. It doesn't make your situation any better.

And it can affect your disposition toward other people. Because some people fail you, you think everyone else will fail you. People will always be people. There will always be good people and there will always be bad people. But if you close your eyes waiting for bad people to pass by, you won't know when good people will also pass by. It was people that caused Joseph to suffer years of affliction. And when time came for God to promote him, He sent people his way. That people hurt your feelings during your crisis is no reason to refrain from everyone around you or take out your frustration on everyone.

Don't let the bad ones keep you from enjoying the good ones. Don't turn yourself into a slave of someone else's malicious insolence. Help the man who hurt you. Embrace the sister who pushed you away. Bless the brother who cursed you. Smile at the person who yelled on you. Pray for the supervisor who disparaged you. Assist the friend who condemned you. If there's anyone you need to forgive, set that person free so God can set you free. Even if you're still having those life struggles, go ahead and forgive those who offend you anyway. Remember, Jesus forgave His killers while He was still hanging on the cross.

Do anything humanly possible to ease or cease the suffering

Count it all joy, my brothers, when you fall into various temptations, knowing that the testing of your faith produces endurance. Let endurance have its perfect work, that you may be perfect and complete, lacking in nothing.
James 1:2-4

I'm yet to meet one person who is happy during affliction, suffering, and hard times. Even Christ, though He knew what was coming, prayed three times in Gethsemane that the cup of sorrow be removed. And on the cross, He cried, "My God, my God, why hast thou forsaken me?" (Matthew 27:46). It was a cry of anguish, pain, and, agony. Yet, He endured it all, not because He could not save Himself, but simply to save us from destruction.

But relative to our own sufferings and afflictions, there are times that the problem can be eased or ceased, from human perspective. We shall consider the following tough situations.

Barrenness is an affliction. By the time a couple starts counting years after marriage, people will be asking questions. But in some cases, barrenness can be reversed by medical procedure.

Several years ago, I knew two sisters who were trusting God for children. Incidentally, they both had the same medical condition—fibroid. Anyone familiar with this condition knows that fibroid hinders pregnancy. But if removed, the woman will be able to conceive. One sister readily agreed to have it removed. Within three years after the surgery, she had two kids. The other sister refused because, according to her, if God wanted her to have kids, then He should remove the fibroid Himself, so He could take all the glory. The last I knew of her, she was still barren. Two sisters in Christ, same affliction, but contrasting dispositions to surgical corrective procedure.

I believe in divine healing. But I also believe God can use doctors to achieve His purpose in my life. That fibroid is surgically removed doesn't mean the doctors get the glory. A team of doctors and nurses worked on me to remove an ectopic pregnancy. But God took all the glory for saving me from what could have turned out fatal. Don't let your rigid mindset stand in the way of your miracle. God can save us using humans as agents, but He'll still take all the glory.

Financial crisis can become an affliction, if not promptly addressed. But it can be a result of imprudent spending—addictive shopping, gambling, lavish lifestyle, and unchecked benevolence, which is uncontrolled generosity. While it's good to be generous, it's wise to know when your generosity is being exploited or when you're overdoing it to your own detriment. That you want to ease someone's burden doesn't mean you create a burden for yourself. Saving someone's head by losing yours is foolishness, not kindness. Don't be so generous that you have little or nothing left to live on. Don't be a giver to the extent you become a beggar.

How about credit cards? Those little plastics are demonized wallet companions. Yes, it feels good to have them, but they're terrible pocket drainers. If you're not careful, they can plunge you into an abyss of financial mess that will require special prayers to pull you out from, and it may take years before you fully recover. Please, don't bring that affliction on yourself. If you're there already, do your best, not just to get out, but to stay out of it.

Some people are stuck in bad marriages. Each day seems like climbing steps to the top of Golgotha to a definite, agonizing death. Except on grounds of infidelity (Matthew 19:9), I'll never advocate divorce. But no law says Christian couples can't separate.

There are Christian brothers who beat their wives. Hard to believe, but true. Once the relationship turns abusive—in any form—I think one spouse needs to save his (her) head. Many spouses, wives more than husbands, are going through hell behind the façade of a happy marriage. They endure unthinkable suffering because they don't want people to see the clearer picture of their miserable relationship.

In some cases, both are saved, and they know the Bible from cover to cover. But just because a person is informed in the Word doesn't imply he's transformed by the Word. Satan knows the entire Bible. Would you be willing to marry him? His knowing the Bible doesn't make him any less evil. I know prayer can still the storm of any bad marriage. But it may take being apart from each other for a while for that to happen. Always remember that the devil is easier kept out than kicked out. Once he takes his roots in the relationship, it may be impossible to undo his damages.

Some spouses wait till one of them snaps and hurts the other, sometimes fatally. Please don't get mad to the point you give the devil a chance and hurt each other. If you feel your life is in danger, do what Jesus did (John 7:1). Distance yourself from the hostile environment. Issues can be resolved only if both of you are alive.

What spiritual battles are you fighting right now? At home, at work, your health, your marriage, your finances? Now, think of what you can do, humanly possible, to either lessen or stop that problem. You may have to part with people whose presence brings bad luck. When Jonah got in the boat going to Tarshish, the Bible says, "There was a mighty tempest in the sea, so that the ship was like to be broken." But soon as the mariners threw him out, "the sea ceased from her raging" (Jonah 1).

There are destiny helpers, and there are destiny destroyers. A person may be carrying a spell and not know it. Everything is okay with you until that person shows up in your life. Before you realize it, regression sets in and you're left wondering and asking why. If you experience that, it's time to throw Jonah out of the boat of your life. Roll away the stone of evil, of bad luck, of danger, and of affliction, so you can enjoy your freedom in Christ. Get rid of them before they end your life. It may not be easy, but you've got to do what you've got to do, so you don't become a partaker of someone else's evil destiny.

And sometimes, the problem is psychosomatic. Too many people are bound by self-imposed yokes. They can't get out of their suffering because, in their minds, that's the way it's supposed to be. It's a family thing and everybody in their generation has had the same problem. Well, just because others in your lineage have it doesn't mean you should have it too. Would you be willing to live the rest of your life blind because blindness runs in your family?

Get that destructive mentality out of your head. Ask God to

help you break free of any thought that will make you settle for less than good. And I know that very soon, you will heave a sigh of relief, in Jesus' Name.

Don't despise strangers

I read an article about a lady who had battled kidney disease for years. It got to the stage that she needed a kidney transplant to save her life. From the look of things, that seemed like a hopeless case for many reasons, but mainly the long waiting period for a donor match.

As the Lord would have it, another lady happened to be in the vicinity of the hospital where she was being treated. The lady heard about it and took interest. Though strangers to each other, she volunteered to donate one of

The stranger you despise may be God's angel sent to save you from the storm. Remember that good Samaritans come in all colors, sizes, and shapes.

her kidneys to save the sick lady's life. When the tests were done, it was a perfect match. And in a short amount of time, the sick was back on her feet. God used a total stranger to save the life of a total stranger. Be careful not to despise strangers, especially during crisis. If you do, you may be shortchanging yourself of God's miracle for your deliverance.

The Bible tells us not to forget "to entertain strangers: for thereby some have entertained angels unawares" (Hebrews 13:2).

- Abraham received the promised child because he entertained strangers (Genesis 18).

- God used a stranger—the good Samaritan—to help the man going from Jerusalem to Jericho, who was attacked by robbers, stripped naked, beaten, and left for half-dead (Luke 10).

- The widow of Zarephath and prophet Elijah were strangers to each other. God used the widow to provide food for the prophet in time of famine. And in reverse, He used the prophet to end lack in the widow's life (1 Kings 16).

- When the Shunammite woman entertained a stranger—prophet Elisha—she was blessed with a child, bringing a permanent end to her barrenness (2 Kings 4).

- A stranger gave water to Jesus at Jacob's well (John 4).

- In 1997, on a dark night, two strangers took us home after our car broke down. It was a help that I'll never forget.

Whoever God sends your way in time of need, accept him (her) without reservations. Do not despise strangers.

Don't look down on anyone

God can send help to us through the most unlikely source. He can delegate anyone as His agent to help us in time of need and fulfill His purpose in our lives. In 2 Kings, we read about Naaman. He wasn't just a great captain in the Syrian army; he was also a man of God. But sadly, he was a leper.

Now Naaman, captain of the host of the king of Syria, was a great man with his master, and honourable, because by him the Lord had given deliverance unto Syria: he was also a mighty man in valour, but he was a leper.
2 Kings 5:1

In most cultures, lepers are outcasts and they're confined to secluded locations, far from normal people. But by virtue of his rank in the army, Naaman lived among his country's social elites. He was nonetheless a leper. But, who would have thought that the solution to his affliction would come through an ordinary little maid that was captured during one of his victorious missions?

The Syrians had gone out in bands, and had brought away captive out of the land of Israel a little maiden; and she waited on Naaman's wife. She said to her mistress, "I wish that my lord were with the prophet who is in Samaria! Then he would heal him of his leprosy." Someone went in, and told his lord, saying, "The maiden who is from the land of Israel said this."
2 Kings 5:2-4, WEB

When Naaman was told about the little maid's suggestion, he didn't contend the suggestion or disparage the maid. That was his first victory. His second victory came through his servants. When Naaman got to Samaria, rather than going out to meet him in person, Elisha simply sent a messenger, "saying, Go and wash in Jordan seven times, and thy flesh shall come again to thee, and thou shalt be clean" (2 Kings 5:10-14).

An ordinary prophet asked a whole army captain and second-in-command to the king, to go and wash in a dirty river when there were cleaner rivers in Damascus? To Naaman, that was an insult. But God used his servants to convince him to obey the prophet, which turned out to be a blessing.

Had he not listened to his wife's maid to go to prophet Elisha, and, had he despised his servants' plight to do as the prophet said, he would have died a leper. God can use anyone to achieve His purpose in your life.

- He used Joseph's ex-inmate to link Joseph to King Pharaoh (Genesis 40).

- He used Rahab, a harlot, to save the lives of His two servants from death (Joshua 2).

- He used David, an ordinary shepherd boy, to save the Israelites from Goliath (1 Samuel 17).

- He used Esther, an orphaned captive girl from Jerusalem, to save the Jewish race from destruction by Haman (Esther 5-9).

- Simon of Cyrene, a commoner, helped Jesus carry His cross to Golgotha (Matthew 27).

- John the beloved, one of the twelve disciples, became Mary's caregiver after Jesus was gone (John 19).

While going through difficult season, please don't profile anybody that God sends your way. And don't limit God with your preconceived mindset of the kind of help He should send. Though you're a believer, He can use an unbeliever to help you achieve your destiny. As an old person, He can use a small child to get you out of your predicament. As a teacher, He can choose one of your students to be your angel in your time of need. As a pastor, that member that you have no regard for, may actually be God's answer to what you've been praying about for years. God can use a person of any color to save a person of any color.

Refrain from ungodly advice

Years back, while going through our immigration process, life was so tough that we listened to anyone with any suggestion. One Sunday afternoon, a lady invited us to her house because she wanted to advise us on how to get through the trillion immigration red tapes and protocols. Coming from someone who was already an American citizen, we gladly accepted her invitation. Within minutes of listening to her, we knew that her good advice was actually a lecture on how to circumvent the proper route. Not to appear rude, we let her finish, thanked her, and left. But her suggestions were quickly discarded. We're children of God and we would not compromise our faith just to live in another country.

It wasn't easy getting through that period. In fact, it took much longer before we became citizens. But we remained faithful throughout because we were "persuaded, that neither death, nor life, nor angels, nor principalities, nor powers, nor things present, nor things to come, Nor height, nor depth, nor any other creature, shall be able to separate us from the love of God, which is in Christ Jesus our Lord" (Romans 8:38-39). At His own appointed time, God honored our faith.

While it's not good to look down on anyone or despise a stranger, you also have to be careful whose advice or suggestions you take. I know that hard times will make a person welcome all kinds of advice and suggestions. But just as God can use any means to help you during your affliction, Satan can use any means to hurt you during your affliction. And one way he does that is to barrage you with ungodly ideas, directly from people around you. *Do this, don't do that. Go to that doctor. Don't go there. Marry another spouse. Don't divorce your spouse. Talk to your pastor. Hey, don't try it. You don't want the whole church hearing about your problem.*

Some may claim "being led by the spirit" to give you a message. And because you're already in a confused state of mind, the messages and suggestions only deepen the confusion. I don't have issues with anyone being led by the spirit, but I want to know what kind of "spirit" is leading the person. The Bible warns us to "believe not every spirit, but try the spirits whether they are of God: because many false prophets are gone out into the world" (1 John 4:1).

Many of those good advisers are honey-tongued destiny

destroyers, Satan's servants who are disguised to appear like agents of light (2 Corinthians 11:14-15). You must be able to discern between good and evil, right and wrong, genuine and fake, true and false.

Like the advice of Sarah to Abraham, to have a child by Hagar the housemaid (Genesis 16), the adviser may mean well, but the advice clearly contradicts biblical principle. And if you follow suit, it can easily derail your train of faith. You hear it and your present condition makes it sound alright. You go for it before realizing it's nothing but Satan's trap. Sometimes, the mistake can be rectified; other times, it may be the birth of a nightmare that you have to live with for the rest of your life.

Because you've been in that ordeal for a long time and there appears no end in sight, people will be quick to offer unbiblical solutions that won't help, but only make your situation worse. Be careful. Don't let anyone push you to do anything that contradicts God's Word. Don't ask for prayer from anyone who prays in any name other than the Name of Jesus (1 Thessalonians 3:3). And don't seek spiritual direction from anyone who doesn't know the Way (John 14:6).

Don't make hasty vows

It's not uncommon for people to vow during trials, like Hannah did before she had Samuel (1 Samuel 1:11). People still do the same thing today. *Lord, if you do this for me, I'll do this in return to show my gratitude.* And that's not a bad idea. In fact, I think it's a wonderful idea. But the problem is, many receive their miracles and forget their vows. And some make vows before realizing that the vows are made in haste.

And Jephthah vowed a vow unto the Lord, and said, If thou shalt without fail deliver the children of Ammon into mine hands, Then it shall be, that whatsoever cometh forth of the doors of my house to meet me, when I return in peace from the children of Ammon, shall surely be the Lord's, and I will offer it up for a burnt offering. So Jephthah passed over unto the children of Ammon to fight against them; and the Lord delivered them into his hands. . . . And Jephthah came to Mizpeh unto his house, and, behold, his daughter came out to meet him with timbrels and with dances: and she was his only child; beside her he had neither son nor daughter. And it came to pass, when he saw her, that he rent his clothes, and said, Alas, my daughter! thou hast brought me very low, and thou art one of them that trouble me: for I have opened my mouth unto the Lord, and I cannot go back.
Judges 11:30-35

He vowed to sacrifice "whatsoever cometh forth of the doors of my house to meet me." Then he blamed his daughter for his mistake. What was he expecting? A goat? A chicken? A lizard? If someone other than his daughter had come out of his house, an innocent person would have died because of his hasty and irrational vow. That vow brought a greater calamity on him than the cause for which he vowed.

Out of eight barren women in the Bible—Sarah (Genesis 21), Rebekah (Genesis 25), Rachel (Genesis 30), Samson's mother (Judges 13), Hannah (1 Samuel 1), Michal (2 Samuel 6), the Shunammite woman (2 Kings 4), and Elisabeth (Luke 1)—only Hannah made a vow while praying for a child. Yet, all but Michal had children before they died, an evil that she brought upon herself.

I've made vows before and nothing happened. And I've experienced many miracles in my life without making any vows. Before you vow, stop, think, and pray. Don't make a vow that you won't be able to fulfill, or such that you will regret for life. We can't use vows to bribe God. He will only do what He wants to do. A vow is a covenant. Once made, forever binding.

If a man vow a vow unto the LORD, or swear an oath to bind his soul with a bond; he shall not break his word, he shall do according to all that proceedeth out of his mouth.
Numbers 30:2

When thou shalt vow a vow unto the LORD thy God, thou shalt not slack to pay it: for the LORD thy God will surely require it of thee; and it would be sin in thee.
Deuteronomy 23:21

Don't be rash with your mouth, and don't let your heart be hasty to utter anything before God; for God is in heaven, and you on earth. Therefore let your words be few. For as a dream comes with a multitude of cares, so a fool's speech with a multitude of words. When you vow a vow to God, don't defer to pay it; for he has no pleasure in fools. Pay that which you vow. It is better that you

should not vow, than that you should vow and not pay. Don't allow your mouth to lead you into sin.
Ecclesiastes 5:2-6, WEB

If you forget your vow, God doesn't. I'm not discrediting vows as bad or unnecessary. But the decision to vow or not to vow should be well thought through before making it. May your trials never push you to say anything that you will regret for the rest of your life, in Jesus' Name.

Let God be God

Few years ago, I proctored a Praxis Exam that lasted about seven hours for three different tests. After the last paper, a guy walked over to me, sweating and obviously distraught. Before I asked what the problem was, he started pouring out his frustration. He said he thought he was well prepared. But he was disappointed at his performance and wasn't sure how it would turn out. On and on he went.

When he finished, I asked if he studied for the exam. He said he did. Then I expressed my candid opinion: That, as human beings, when we have done what we need to do, we start fretting over what only God can do, as if He needs our help to accomplish His goals and purposes in our lives. Since he did everything he was supposed to do to pass the exam, including sitting for hours, I asked him to relax and let God do what only God could do. He looked at me and said no one has ever been that real with him. A big relief came over him and his countenance changed immediately. The guy that walked over to me sad left my presence glad, gleeful, and hopeful.

In the Garden of Gethsemane, Jesus was so overcome by grief that He asked God to spare Him the cup of sorrow. Then, almost like taking back His words, He told God that only His will be done. That was Jesus letting God be God.

As a child of God, I really wish I understand why God acts the way He does, sometimes. But the more I try to understand Him, the more confused I get. Then I remember His omnipotence, His loving kindness, His omniscience, and His infallible, ever abiding presence. I remember the tough times He has brought me through. Then I reassure myself that if He didn't fail me then, He won't fail me now. Though things may look bad from human perspective, it's all good from God's perspective. And even if He chooses not to answer my prayer the way I wish, it doesn't change the fact that He's God, and He always will be God.

In any situation or circumstance that you find yourself, always let God be God.

What to do after Calvary crisis

Give thanks

And whatsoever ye do in word or deed, do all in the name of the Lord Jesus, giving thanks to God and the Father by him.
Colossians 3:17

People condemn the Israelites for being so ungrateful after their deliverance from Egypt. Those people were full of it. For over four hundred years, they cried and begged God to deliver them from Pharaoh's bondage. When that happened, rather than be grateful for the long-awaited freedom, they welcomed it with the most abhorrent attitude, nagging and complaining right from the onset of their departure from Egypt.

And they said unto Moses, Because there were no graves in Egypt, hast thou taken us away to die in the wilderness? wherefore hast thou dealt thus with us, to carry us forth out of Egypt? Is not this the word that we did tell thee in Egypt, saying, Let us alone, that we may serve the Egyptians? For it had been better for us to serve the Egyptians, than that we should die in the wilderness.
Exodus 14:11-12

For the forty years of their wilderness merry-go-round, it was miracle upon miracle—both of protection and provision. Yet, not a single moment of reflection, either to thank God or Moses. The truth is, many of us are like that. Once we receive the miracle, we forget the miracle worker. There are folks who pray for years for a miracle and it never happens. So, when you receive one, don't you think it's worth thanking God for? It's not like God has a shortage of grateful children thanking Him every moment of the day. But when we give thanks for one blessing, we're sure to receive another one, a fact made apparent in the healing of the ten lepers.

*And it came to pass, as he went to Jerusalem, that he passed through the midst of Samaria and Galilee. And as he entered into a certain village, there met him ten men that were lepers, which stood afar off: And they lifted up their voices, and said, Jesus, Master, have mercy on us. And when he saw them, he said unto them, Go shew yourselves unto the priests. And it came to pass, that, as they went, they were cleansed. And one of them, when he saw that he was healed, turned back, and with a loud voice glorified God, And fell down on his face at his feet, giving him thanks: and he was a Samaritan. And Jesus answering said, **Were there not ten cleansed? but where are the nine?** There are not found that returned to give glory to God, save this stranger. And he said unto him, Arise, go thy way: thy faith hath made thee whole.*
Luke 17:11-19 (Emphasis mine)

Was Jesus complaining about the nine lepers who didn't return to thank Him? No! He was just using the incident to teach us an attitude of gratitude at all times, and especially after a miracle, which could be anything from healing to promotion. As parents, when our children thank us for things, we're encouraged to do more. As our Father, God feels the same way. He's happy when we return to thank Him for things, and that encourages Him to do more. We don't have to wait till we receive a big miracle before giving thanks, and we don't have to delay our thanksgiving till Thanksgiving Day. For a child of God, every day is Thanksgiving day because there's always something to thank God for, every day.

Giving thanks always for all things unto God and the Father in the name of our Lord Jesus Christ.
Ephesians 5:20

If I were to go by my present situation, I won't be writing about giving thanks. But when I think of the provision God had made ready even before the problem, I cannot but thank Him, a million times over. Read what He says.

*There hath no temptation taken you **(me)** but such as is common to man: but God is faithful, who will not suffer you **(me)** to be tempted above that ye are **(I am)** able; but will with the temptation also make a way to escape, that ye **(I)** may be able to bear it.*
1 Corinthians 10:13 *(Emphases mine)*

God knew about this season of my life before it came. And He already worked it out, leaving me with nothing but praises and thanksgiving to offer unto Him. [Thank You Daddy God.]

Don't underestimate the power of thanksgiving. When God delivers you out of a crisis, don't be like the Israelites or the nine lepers. Be like the one leper who returned to give thanks. And remember to thank those who help you during your difficult times. It doesn't mean you give a gift in return, like Naaman tried to do for Elisha after he was cured of leprosy (2 Kings 5:15-19). If you can afford it, that's okay. But don't feel compelled to. I'm sure just saying, *Thank you*, will mean a lot to whoever helps you in time of need.

Rejoice

Closely related to giving thanks is rejoicing after your miracle. Though they sound similar, but they're different. A person can give thanks and no one will know about it. But when you rejoice, people will know that you're happy because you will be making a joyful noise unto the Lord (Psalm 66:1).

David says, "I will praise thee, O LORD, with my whole heart; I will shew forth all thy marvellous works. I will be glad and rejoice in thee: I will sing praise to thy name, O thou most High" (Psalm 9:1-2). Rejoicing is uncontainable.

There are numerous instances in the Bible when people rejoiced, either after a miracle or deliverance from enemies. But none inspires me like that of the man born lame, who begged for alms at the entrance to the temple.

Now Peter and John went up together into the temple at the hour of prayer, being the ninth hour. And a certain man lame from his mother's womb was carried, whom they laid daily at the gate of

the temple which is called Beautiful, to ask alms of them that entered into the temple; Who seeing Peter and John about to go into the temple asked an alms. And Peter, fastening his eyes upon him with John, said, Look on us. And he gave heed unto them, expecting to receive something of them. Then Peter said, Silver and gold have I none; but such as I have give I thee: In the name of Jesus Christ of Nazareth rise up and walk. And he took him by the right hand, and lifted him up: and immediately his feet and ankle bones received strength. And he leaping up stood, and walked, and entered with them into the temple, walking, and leaping, and praising God. And all the people saw him walking and praising God: And they knew that it was he which sat for alms at the Beautiful gate of the temple: and they were filled with wonder and amazement at that which had happened unto him. And as the lame man which was healed held Peter and John, all the people ran together unto them in the porch that is called Solomon's, greatly wondering.
Acts 3:1-11

Do you know that praise is magnetic? When people see you praising and rejoicing, there's a divine gravitational pull towards you. Somehow, they get curious and want to know the reason for your joy. That was what happened in the above passage. All the years that the *certain* man had been begging for alms, he never attracted crowd. The only attention he drew to himself was for people to give him money. But after his miracle, he couldn't contain the joy. Oh my goodness. That guy went nuts.

Do you blame him? He was over forty years and had never walked in his life (Acts 4:22). So when he got up for the first time, he made sure to let everyone know that the bondage was broken, that God had set him free, that he didn't need to be carried like a baby anymore, that the days of laying him down at the gate of the temple were over, that he no longer constituted an ugly sight at the beautiful gate, that people could keep their money because he had been transported from, *he which sat*, to *the man who walked*. He didn't even wait for invitation before following Peter and John inside the temple.

And Peter quickly took advantage of his rejoicing to tell the curious crowd about the power of the One in Whose Name the lame man was *walking, and leaping, and praising God*. He left home a beggar and returned home a believer.

Has God answered your prayer? Have you received a miracle? Then join me as I sing.

What the Lord has done for me, I cannot tell it all
What the Lord has done for me, I cannot tell it all
What the Lord has done for me, I cannot tell it all
He saved me, and washed me in His blood.

So I can shout Halleluyah
I can shout Halleluyah
I can shout, praise the Lord
So I can shout Halleluyah
I can shout Halleluyah
I can shout, praise the Lord (Anonymous).

Don't forget to give thanks. But after that, rejoice and let the world know what the Lord has done for you.

Forget your bitter past

Brethren, I count not myself to have apprehended: but this one thing I do, forgetting those things which are behind, and reaching forth unto those things which are before, I press toward the mark for the prize of the high calling of God in Christ Jesus.
Philippians 3:13-14

Just by listening to people tell their stories, it's obvious that many lives are plagued by past hurts resulting from several things. For some, those hurts have lasted years, creating a lingering and emotional torture they will struggle with for a very long time, if not forever. If that applies to you, please let go, so you can enjoy your life.

But I also like to address this topic from other perspectives different from the above. The first deals with the nasty experiences that a person suffers from other people during a difficult season. We know what happened to Sarah, Hannah, Job, Joseph, and Jesus. While going through affliction, they endured insults, ridicule, and painful treatment from people, even at the peak of their suffering. But none of them held on to their past hurts.

• Before Sarah had Isaac, Hagar despised her (Genesis 16:4). But once she had Isaac, she didn't let Hagar's past evil attitude keep her from enjoying her bundle of joy.

• Before Samuel was born, Peninnah was a thorn in Hannah's flesh (1 Samuel 1:6). But after she had Samuel, Hannah forgot about Peninnah, and instead, concentrated on her son.

- Because of envy, Joseph's brothers made him suffer for years in a strange land. But after becoming prime minister in Egypt, he let go of all the hurts from his brothers or anyone else. In fact, he named his firstborn Manasseh, "For God, said he, hath made me forget all my toil, and all my father's house" (Genesis 41:51).

On another realm, you must forget your bitter past by not concentrating on lost years. When Abraham had Isaac at hundred years old, all he did was rejoice at the birth of the promised child, putting behind him the donkey's years of waiting and trusting. They were gone and gone forever.

You should have received your College degree forty years ago. Graduating at this age means walking the stage with children the same age as your grandchildren. And may I ask, so what? Whatever caused the delay,

When you waste your energy brooding over past failures, pains, and disappointments, you'll have no energy left to enjoy your blessings when they come.

forget it and enjoy your newly acquired knowledge. There are thousands who wish they can do the same thing. But death made it impossible for them. Many who're alive lacked the means then, and still lack the means now. You're alive and have the means to accomplish what they couldn't and still can't accomplish. That alone should make you happy.

Lastly, forget the bitter past by forgiving yourself. I know some past actions have irrevocable consequences. You wake up every day wishing you had done things differently. Well, the deed is done and there's nothing you can do about it. So, instead of spending years menacing and crying over spilled milk, get up and think of other ways you can live a positive life, to your benefit and that of others around you. Refuse to stay a victim of your past and release yourself from its lethal effects. If God says He has forgiven you, you need to forgive yourself.

Encourage those in crisis

I've shared this testimony before, and I will continue to do so till His kingdom comes. The year was 2000, in Columbus, Ohio. For four years, life had been very difficult. Speaking of a test of faith in almost every area of our life, particularly finances. Then it seemed like we had a breakthrough. My husband got a job in a company in Lima, Ohio. Our joy was beyond measure as he went and resumed work, as in a real job. But four days later, he was sent back home due to immigration red tapes. Our joy instantly turned into sorrow and confusion.

How can God do this? Is He punishing us for an unknown sin? Does He even care about us anymore? No answer.

Back then, we attended Christian Assembly in Columbus. The following Sunday after service, I called one of my dear sisters in Christ, Sandra Gist, and poured my heart out to her. As we walked toward her car, she listened without interrupting. After encouraging me the best way she could, she capped it with this: *Don't worry, Foye. If God has gone this far, He won't back out.* I stood there frozen, while she drove off.

It was what I needed to hear. I immediately remembered the Israelites at the Red Sea, how they panicked because they thought God would watch them drown in the Sea, and fail on His promise to take them to the Promised Land. My hope was renewed and I held on to that faith-reviving statement. And God didn't back out till the process was complete. Three months later, my husband returned to work. Though things looked bad and the three months seemed like forever, we held tight to the promise that He who began the good work would complete it (Philippians 1:6).

A strong faith can become weak under pressure if a problem persists for too long. Sometimes, it's like the more the person prays, the worse things get. And with each passing day, the faith gets weaker. At such moment, simple encouragement from others can go a long way to ease the pain. The Bible asks us to "exhort one another, and build each other up" (1 Thessalonians 5:11, WEB) and to "exhort one another daily" (Hebrews 3:13).

To exhort is to encourage. If you can't do it daily, do it when someone you know is having problems. Let the person know that you're praying for him (her), that everything will be okay, that God is working things out and He'll come through very soon. Ask if there's something he (she) needs or any help you can render. It doesn't have to be a big help, but it's help. If you have a good idea or suggestion, even if it's the bitter truth, share it.

I know they say truth hurts. I think that depends on how it's presented. Admonition is different from condemnation. Admonish, but don't condemn. Remember that the words you speak may be the key that will unlock the closed door of faith in the individual's life.

Help those in crisis

As Jesus was dragged to Golgotha, He became weak and His already heavy cross got heavier. Then something dramatic happened. A man named Simon of Cyrene helped our Savior carry the cross. Matthew and Mark both claim that Simon was compelled to carry the cross for Jesus. Luke says he was laid hold upon, more like grabbing him by the shoulder (Matthew 27:32; Mark 15:21; Luke 23:26). Did he have any chance to decline? Or, was he too scared to do so, not wanting the same fate to befall him as the Man whose cross he would be carrying? Nobody knows.

But whether he was forced to carry Jesus' cross or he did so voluntarily, the bottom line is that Simon rendered assistance to Jesus when He was frail and helpless. No account of how long or how far he carried the Lord's cross. Five minutes? Ten minutes? Half a mile? One mile? Most likely, he carried it the rest of the crowded and dusty *Via Dolorosa* to Golgotha's top. Whatever the time or distance, that simple kindness was a relief to Jesus. Isn't that what helping others is all about?

You can help someone going through crisis by rendering any assistance to lighten the person's burden. A ride to work or doctor's appointment, free groceries, lawn mowing, mail picking, even little chores around the house, if you trust the person.

While in Capernaum, a paralytic was brought to Jesus by four people, which Luke clarifies as four men (Luke 5:18).

When he entered again into Capernaum after some days, it was heard that he was in the house. . . . Four people came, carrying a paralytic to him. When they could not come near to him for the crowd, they removed the roof where he was. When they had broken it up, they let down the mat that the paralytic was lying on. Jesus, seeing their faith, said to the paralytic, "Son, your sins are forgiven you." . . . "I tell you, arise, take up your mat, and go to your house." He arose, and immediately took up the mat, and went out in front of them all; so that they were all amazed, and glorified God, saying, "We never saw anything like this!"
Mark 2:1-12, WEB

The man's paralysis was a heavy cross and a mountainous climb. The four men could walk, but the paralytic could not. So, they took it upon themselves to render whatever assistance they could to lessen his burden, so he too could enjoy the freedom of movement that they had enjoyed their entire life. And if they had to tear the roof of someone's house to achieve their purpose, so be it. It was a single move that ended the paralytic's affliction.

When we tell others about Jesus, let's back it up with good deeds to make the sermon more meaningful to them.

What good is it, my brothers, if a man says he has faith, but has no works? Can faith save him? And if a brother or sister is naked and in lack of daily food, and one of you tells them, "Go in peace, be warmed and filled"; and yet you didn't give them the things the body needs, what good is it? Even so faith, if it has no works, is dead in itself.
James 2:14-17, WEB

Till this day, the love we received at Christian Assembly remains an indelible part of our life. During those struggling years, church members, and especially Pastor Sam Farina, made sure that we were okay. From free enrollment for my boys at the Church's elementary school (Charisma Academy), to the provision of basic needs, to financial assistance, name it. And after we left, Pastor

If you can't walk the talk, don't talk the walk. Don't preach how to live if you don't live what you preach.

Sam continued to check on us. He didn't just preach love and compassion, he lived a life full of love and compassion for everybody. And for my family, his love preaches on.

Directly or indirectly, helping someone in need creates an emotional bond between the helper and the helped. In fact, you may never meet or see each other again; but the person you helped will remember that gesture for a long, long time. The Bible says, "Don't say to your neighbor, "Go, and come again; tomorrow I

91

will give it to you," when you have it by you (Proverbs 3:28-29, WEB). In other words, if you can help now, don't delay till later.

When was the last time you helped somebody? A struggling neighbor, a sick church member, a child whose winter coat is worn out, but the parents can't afford a new one. When it comes to rendering assistance, the choices are endless.

Your faith is good. But if you don't care about others, it's not good enough to get that message of hope across as intended. There's no point claiming to be so spirit filled, yet so void of love and compassion.

Share your testimony

Blessed be the God and Father of our Lord Jesus Christ, the Father of mercies and God of all comfort; who comforts us in all our affliction, that we may be able to comfort those who are in any affliction, through the comfort with which we ourselves are comforted by God.
2 Corinthians 1:3-4

I knew a man who suffered chronic neck pain for fifteen years, non-stop. He did everything humanly possible, but nothing worked. While narrating his ordeal, he said he swung his neck so much, it became a subconscious habit. And there were days he couldn't move or turn his neck at all. At some point, the illness became a devourer as he spent everything to get healed, like the woman with the issue of blood. Yet, the pain persisted.

Then one day, as he turned his television on, he stumbled on a Christian station. As a Muslim, his immediate inclination was to change the channel. But that day, something told him to set his religion aside and listen to the preacher as he talked about faith in Jesus. After the message, the preacher asked people to lay hands on any area of their body where there was pain, and to believe that there's no barrier that prayer cannot penetrate, be it distance or technology.

Well, he placed his hand on his neck but nothing happened. Disappointed but not surprised, he went to bed. When he woke up the next morning, he realized he had slept through the entire night, something he hadn't done in fifteen years. The pain had *vamoosed,* gone without a trace.

From that moment, he was unstoppable, ready to go any distance to share his testimony and to tell others about the Man called Jesus. Persecution from the other religion? You bet. But for all he cared, that was nothing compared to what he suffered for fifteen years. His miracle is a testimony of the healing power in the Name of Jesus. Testimonies strengthen the faith of the hearer/s.

• Sarah and Elizabeth both had babies at very old age. That's a testimony that no womb is so dead that God can't make alive again (Genesis 21; Luke 1).

• Joseph's promotion from prison to palace is a testimony that God can take you from the valley of absolute sorrow and set you on the mountain of abounding joy (Genesis 41).

• The parting of the Red Sea is a testimony that God can make a way where there's no way (Exodus 14).

• The drowning of Pharaoh's army in the Red Sea is a testimony that God will deal with those enemies that won't leave us alone (Exodus 14).

▪ The deliverance of the three Hebrew teenagers from fire is a testimony that God will deliver His children out of any frightening situation (Daniel 3).

▪ The salvation of the thief on the cross is a testimony that God will save anyone who repents and returns to Him (Luke 23).

▪ Paul's conversion, after years of persecuting Christians, is a testimony that no heart is that stony that God cannot melt (Acts 9).

If you know anyone in crisis and it's something you can relate to, or you know someone who traveled the same road and made it out successfully, share it with the person currently going through that crisis.

For a situation like financial crisis, maybe there was a time when you were deep in debt. Now you're debt-free. But you know someone in the same dilemma. Share your experience with the person, what you did differently to get out of debt. Not everything requires sleepless intercession or divine intervention. Sometimes, all it takes is changing your action to change your situation. If we can learn from our mistakes, we won't repeat them.

When you share your story, please do so with humility. Taking the glory for your story indirectly means God has nothing to do with it. That's spiritual arrogance, which will only produce a negative effect on the hearer. A struggling person has a lot on his (her) mind and the last thing he (she) needs is a narcissist, whose self-glorifying testimony is more confusing than convincing.

And please don't use your testimony to condemn or judge anyone. If you have nothing good to say to a person in pain, try saying nothing. Even when you know that the person is to blame for the problem, hold your criticism till a much later time or hold it forever.

Tell others about the love of Jesus

As you tell people about the power in the Name of Jesus, don't forget to tell them about His love for mankind. Suffering in this world is like a grain of sand when compared to suffering in eternity. While the former lasts a little while, the latter lasts forever. And as believers in Christ, we're called to preach the gospel and be Christ's ambassadors unto those who don't know Him as Lord and Savior. We can tell them how the love of Jesus transformed our lives, gave us hope in turmoil, and strength in weakness.

Many unsaved souls are struggling with life here on earth. And because they don't know the Savior, they lack the faith to cope with adversity, and have no hope for a better life after this earth. But it'll be easier to tell them about the love of Jesus when we love them the way He loves us. He says, "A new commandment I give unto you, That ye love one another; as I have loved you, that ye also love one another. By this shall all men know that ye are my disciples, if ye have love one to another" (John 13:34-35).

When the saved thief heard Jesus pray for His killers, he sensed an unusual love in Him. Good thing he didn't only sense it, it changed his life for eternity. What can you say about the love of Jesus? Turn it into an evangelism mantra to tell others about Him. Sometimes, it's more effective than preaching from a pulpit.

Pray for those in crisis

Last but not least, pray for anyone you know who is going through trying times, whether you're with them or away from them. It doesn't mean the concerned individual quits praying. It simply means joining your faith with that of the individual for a more effective answer because there's power in agreement.

Again I say unto you, That if two of you shall agree on earth as touching any thing that they shall ask, it shall be done for them of my Father which is in heaven. For where two or three are gathered together in my name, there am I in the midst of them.
Matthew 18:19-20

This isn't about praying for those who prayed for you or

helped you during your own crisis. It's not about those you like or those who like you. It's praying for whoever. Our biggest prayer model is the Lord Himself. Jesus prayed like that was all He was born to do. He prayed before, during, and after anything He did. Even in His time of sorrow and deep agony, Jesus prayed. He tells us to, "Love your enemies, bless them that curse you, do good to them that hate you, and pray for them which despitefully use you, and persecute you" (Matthew 5:44). "Don't rejoice when your enemy falls. Don't let your heart be glad when he is overthrown" (Proverbs 24:17).

I know it hurts when people, especially fellow believers, shy away from helping us during our struggles, not because they can't, but because they don't care. And there are folks who grin from ear to ear just seeing someone they don't like get in trouble. But that's okay. Still pray for them and do so without any grudges.

Foye Adedokun

CALVARY

Calvary, oh blessed Calvary

In Gethsemane with His men, each one asleep like a stone
Sweating and sorrowful, Jesus Christ laid and prayed alone
That were it possible, He, the cup of sorrow could be spared
Yet not His will, but that of His Father be done, He declared
It was a moment when Judas with a kiss, hailed his Master
A man called to be a disciple, but turned out to be a disaster
For thirty pieces of silver, man's Savior was betrayed
Like a slave without worth, God's Son was portrayed
On a glorious Friday in the hours of the morning
A day like any other day, so bright and so sunny
Accused and tried as a traitor, Jesus stood before Pilate
Declared guilty for no just cause, He accepted His fate
With the enemies' whips pounding His body like a storm
His flesh soon in shreds, left like a figure without a form
A heavy cross upon my Lord's shoulder was laid
The heavy load of my sins upon Him was placed
Burdened and sorrowful, He became heavy hearted
The friends He counted on, had all fled and deserted
As He climbed the rugged steps to His place of death
My Savior became very weak and totally out of breath
He wept, He struggled, He pushed, He groaned
He staggered, He fell, He screamed, He moaned
Oh! The tears of His mother as she watched her Son
And the pain of knowing her Son could soon be gone
Thirty-three years earlier, she received a divine visitation
That this her Son would come by Holy Spirit conception
Though nothing at that moment gave her the faintest clue
Yet against all hope she hoped that this could not be true
No way the life of the life Giver would be cheaply taken
No way the strength of the Almighty could be so shaken
She heard the crowd of followers crying, Release Him
And heard the crowd of haters chanting, Crucify Him

She watched His assailants as they hammered and nailed
In their ignorance rejoicing, thinking they had prevailed
"Father, forgive them; for they know not what they do"
He prayed this for His killers, and prayed it for me too
His promise of paradise to a thief on a cross was given
From a second death to be free and all his sins forgiven
For His mother Mary, He called her attention to John
So when He was gone, he would be to her like a son
In a trembling voice Mary heard her Savior pray
In a language unmistakable and clear as the day
To His Father He cried, "Eloi, Eloi, lama sabachthani"
It means, My God, my God, why hast thou forsaken me
But when He remembered for that purpose He was born
He submitted to His Father's will, till the work be done
While the soldiers their lots for His garment they cast
Tired and weary, the Water of life cried out, "I thirst"
Oh! For one act of kindness they should have been eager
But in place of water, they gave Him a sponge of vinegar

Calvary, oh memorable Calvary
Thou beautiful hill of a criminal's salvation
The glorious mount of my own redemption
On you stood the cross that bore my Lord
As He bled and died for the sins of the world
That day on Golgotha broke with daylight so bright
But within hours, darkness turned the light into night
To death till the end my Savior remained humble
Defeating the enemies' wish to make Him stumble
How glorious the moment when the temple veil was torn
And indeed at last, the salvation victory the Lord had won
"It is finished." *Tetelestai*, His mission on earth was finished
The redemption work He came to do was finally accomplished
With the thunderous echo of His voice heard from coast to coast
He commended His spirit to His Father, and gave up the ghost

Foye Adedokun

On you, oh Golgotha, men committed the terrible deicide
As Jesus was murdered, His enemies mocking till He died
Dear Savior, who started His journey on the floor of a manger
Endured life, treated in a manner unbefitting even for a stranger

Calvary, oh glorious Calvary
The enduring tales of nails, of wails, and of clamor
Have lived to tell of your eternal glory and glamour
How high on top of you I long to step and stand
For I know you'll be one view so great and grand
To see the hill where the saved thief's fate was sealed
The hallowed site where mortal saints have kneeled
To step on Golgotha, the hilly ground of death and dread
To see Calvary, where God's love overcame man's hatred
To stand on the spot where my Lord's cross once stood
On that very spot where evil was conquered with good
Calvary, for me you are more than a mountain
My Savior's blood flows still from your fountain
From His spear-pierced veins like a river it gushed
From His thorn-crowned head like water it rushed
For the debt of my sins He was hung on the tree
That I from the pangs of hell 'll be saved and free
Such a love wonderful beyond fathomable
A sacrifice so great with force unstoppable
He died for sinners, and yes, He died on you
And He rose again like He said He would do
He's now in heaven, seated with the Father
But will one day return, His saints to gather
Thank You slain Lamb for Your death on Calvary
Thank You for the blood You shed for the weary
I wish I have what it 'll take to repay the sacrifice
But nothing a wretch like me has can ever suffice
So this salvation race I determine to run with grace
And pray one day to finally see Your glorious face

100

To You this day my Savior, a vow I solemnly make
That when my last breath on this earth I shall take
To Thee my Redeemer, my King, and Lord Most High
I pray my soul shall fly, in that beautiful home in the sky
With patience and courage, help me to stand true and bold
So when my life is o'er, with You I'll walk the streets of gold
Copyright © 2018. Foye Adedokun.

Nothing on earth will compare to seeing Christ in heaven. But it's good to imagine that a glimpse of Calvary may give that feeling of a stray sheep reunited with her Shepherd and Overseer of her soul (1 Peter 2:25). And with that, I move on to the **Cross**, the **Christ**, and, the **Criminals**.

3

The Cross

Looking unto Jesus the author and finisher of our faith; who for the joy that was set before him endured the cross, despising the shame, and is set down at the right hand of the throne of God. For consider him that endured such contradiction of sinners against himself, lest ye be wearied and faint in your minds.
Hebrews 12:2-3

Whereas the cross may be several thousand years old, dating back to pre-Jesus era, its message from the day our Savior was crucified on it has never waxed old. Some artists' impressions, myself included, portray the middle cross, that of Christ, as taller than the ones on both sides, those of the criminals. I don't know if that's reality or pure sentiment.

But sometimes I wonder if the Lord's cross was used or new. If used, did it carry the blood stains of those crucified on it before Him? If so, was it washed clean or left dirty and stinking before hanging Jesus on it? If new, was it randomly picked from the cross shop or specially ordered and custom-made for my Lord? Which carpenter made that particular cross? Did he know whose cross he was making? After Christ, did another criminal die on that cross? If not, did the cross get taken away, stolen, destroyed, kept in a museum somewhere by some unknown folks; or, did it vanish into oblivion, leaving no traces for archaeological rediscovery?

And, were it possible to retrieve it, could it possess some miracle power, like Elisha's bones in 2 Kings 13:21, or, aprons and handkerchiefs from Paul's body in Acts 19:12? So many questions I'd love to ask, but none for which I'll get an answer that will be good enough to satisfy my intellectual curiosity.

However, one thing I know and with certainty declare: That the cross that once stood for condemnation, torture, shame, ridicule, and physical death, now stands for salvation, truth, acceptance, and eternal life. Crucifixion was a common form of execution in those days, and only death can tell how many criminals took their last breaths on the cross. There was nothing good about the cross prior to the crucifixion of Jesus. It was an intimidating object that everybody avoided and nobody embraced.

But on one sunny day, the image of the cross was rebranded, as it stood tall and high on Calvary's top, with Christ's hands and feet nailed deep into it, and He was lifted up from the earth. It was a culmination of events, from the Garden of Gethsemane where He was arrested, to the moment when He breathed His last, gave up the ghost, and perfected the work of redemption for which He was born.

From that point forward, the story of the cross changed

from shame to fame, from disgrace to grace, from terrifying to glorifying, and from horrifying to humbling. The cross now comes in different sizes to hang on doors, display as decorations, or wear as fancy jewelries. To those who don't know any better, Christ's death on the cross marked a shameful end of life. But to the saved and redeemed, the cross is our hope of glory (Colossians 1:27).

Please go along with me and let's consider some vital lessons about the cross.

From an emblem of fear, disgrace, and death, to an emblem of courage, grace, and life

Among the high-profile executions in Nigeria was that of the notorious armed robber, Ishola Oyenusi, who, in an apparent desperation for attention, dubbed himself a doctor—quite a bogus title for a man with zero diction. His level of infamy among the rank and file of vicious and dreaded criminals was underscored by his relaxed grinning to the 1971 execution of him and his gang members. And it remained unmatched until 1987, when a more notorious and merciless armed robber—Lawrence Anini—was executed, along with his criminal comrades.

Many more like them passed through prison hallways into heavily guarded trucks, and took their last rides of life to the popular beach of death, where they were tightly roped to steel drum posts that bore the dark blood stains of their predecessors in crime. As they slowly stepped out of the armored trucks onto the sandy shore, they were cursed, jeered, and derided by thousands of profusely sweating spectators, who had waited in great anticipation. Many, including criminals yet uncaught, stretched their necks to catch a glimpse of the societal hoodlums, before they were bullet-silenced forever, never to be seen, heard, or feared again.

But of the battalion that trooped out to watch them die, ask if anyone would be proud to embrace the execution drum and declare his (her) loyalty to it. I'm sure not a single hand would go up. Though years of public executions have not helped to deter crime in the country, still, no one, not even an armed robber, wants to have anything to do with the execution drums. For years, those drums have stood as formidable ugly sights on a famous beautiful site—the Lagos Bar Beach.

A similar scenario took place on Golgotha, and most likely a common occurrence too, as time after time, criminals were dragged to the hill, nailed to crosses, and sent on their last journeys to eternities of undetermined fate. And just as no one wants to have anything to do with the Lagos Bar Beach execution drums, people in biblical days avoided the cross because it was a symbol of fear, humiliation, ridicule, shame, slow, and painful death. But the day Jesus was crucified, the fate of the cross changed forever. It was the moment when the insurmountable force of light overturned a long existing legacy of darkness.

Two real criminals were executed on Golgotha, each one on a cross. In the middle of the two criminals stood the cross on which Christ our Savior was murdered for His crime of "good deeds." To His killers, that would teach other people an unforgettable lesson, to never believe or profess any faith in that Man called Jesus. But to their shame and to the glory of God, the reverse happened. From that time forward, souls after souls have been picking up their crosses to follow Jesus with an unstoppable determination, lending a better understanding to the charge He gave His disciples.

Saying, The Son of man must suffer many things, and be rejected of the elders and chief priests and scribes, and be slain, and be raised the third day. And he said to them all, If any man will come after me, let him deny himself, and take up his cross daily, and follow me. For whosoever will save his life shall lose it: but whosoever will lose his life for my sake, the same shall save it.
Luke 9:22-24

Followers of Christ all over the world are not scared of the cross because our cross is no longer on Golgotha, but in our hearts. It's not a visible horizontal beam nailed to a visible vertical beam. Rather, it's an invisible, yet obvious sign of unity through Christ's death on the visible cross.

The cross in a believer's life is not a work of carpentry. It's daily self-denial, total submission to God's will, and determination to live a godly life, even at the expense of losing everything for the sake of His kingdom.

And with a force inexorable, a determination irrepressible, and dignity unassailable, we take pride in embracing it, bearing it, and yes, dying for it. For in so doing, we, like Paul, associate with the crucifixion of Jesus and declare, "I am crucified with Christ: nevertheless I live; yet not I, but Christ liveth in me: and the life which I now live in the flesh I live by the faith of the Son of God, who loved me, and gave himself for me" (Galatians 2:20).

We glory in nothing, "save in the cross of our Lord Jesus Christ" (Galatians 6:14). It's nothing about us, but everything about Him because serving Him takes precedence over and above every other thing we hold dear. To take up our cross is to be willing and ready to let go of anything that may hinder us from bearing it daily—relationship, occupation, wealth, status, or our dear lives. And we do so without fear or shame. Anything contrary to that negates what true faith in Christ and the cross stands for, and puts us on the same platform as those who worship carved objects.

As believers, when we glory in the cross, it's not because of the cross itself, but because of Christ who died on the cross. The cross did its job once, on Calvary. After Christ's body was taken down, it's hard to say what happened to the cross. But all believers recognize the death of Christ on the cross as a unifying force that cannot be shaken. And when Christ comes to take us home, there will be no culture, creed, or color, just a body of believers united in Christ by His death on the cross.

For the Lord himself shall descend from heaven with a shout, with the voice of the archangel, and with the trump of God: and the dead in Christ shall rise first: Then we which are alive and remain shall be caught up together with them in the clouds, to meet the Lord in the air: and so shall we ever be with the Lord.
1 Thessalonians 4:16-17

Can you picture the awesomeness of meeting the likes of Abraham, Joseph, Elijah, Elisha, Daniel, Peter, Paul, John, Stephen? Awesome, right? Now, imagine spending eternity with them and with Jesus. To be honest, no comprehensible imagination can do justice to the magnitude of that thought. The last part of the above passage says, "and so shall we ever be with the Lord." Even a thousand years with Him would be thrilling, not to mention forever. And that will be so for as many as pick up the cross to follow Him.

Do you wish to be part of the crew? Why not pick up your cross today? You don't need to go and purchase one from the store. It all happens in your heart. Ask Jesus into your life and continue to live in His will till you see Him in glory. And that's it.

It brought good out of evil

Can there any good thing come out of evil? That sounds like Nathanael asking Philip, "Can there any good thing come out of Nazareth?" (John 1:46). The way a situation looks can make people to prejudge its outcome. A person's current dilemma can make the closest friend, a relative, or the person himself (herself) think everything but a positive result.

At the Red Sea, the Israelites got scared when they "lifted up their eyes, and, behold, the Egyptians marched after them; and they were sore afraid: and the children of Israel cried out unto the LORD" (Exodus 14:10). There was no way forward, and no way backward. Be honest. If you were one of them, wouldn't you be scared? Naturally, they thought they would either drown in the sea or be slaughtered by Pharaoh's army. None of them expected the miracle that followed that ordeal.

Jesus' killers didn't envisage anything good resulting from their evil deed. They were blinded by ignorance. When Jesus died on the cross, they thought they had accomplished their mission. But God thwarted their evil plan when the Man they killed rose again on the third day. His crucifixion marked the beginning of a revival that has captured the entire world by firestorm, as souls in droves get saved every day, and in a magnitude unprecedented by the Golgotha murderers of justice. Christ's blood flows still, washing and cleansing even the dirtiest of sinners.

The joy of their evil mission lasted but a moment. But the joy of the redemption of mankind has lasted since that day, and will last through all eternity. The evil done to my Lord on Calvary is the reason I'm now called a child of God, a redeemed Christian, a follower of Christ, a royal priesthood, and a heavenly pilgrim. Behold the good coming out of evil.

Mercy replaced judgment

With my truckloads of sins, how can I call myself a child of God, a believer, a saved soul, or a heaven-bound pilgrim? What qualities do I possess to put myself in the same category as other saints, living or dead? Sometimes, I wonder if someone is thinking that way about me. And should that be the case, let me use this medium to clear the air.

You see, it's not about me or my sins. In fact, if God had considered my sins, He would never give me a second chance. But glory be unto His holy Name because His mercy far outlasts His judgment. Like apostle Paul, because of His mercy that I received, I was spared the judgment that I deserved.

*And I thank Christ Jesus our Lord, who hath enabled me, for that he counted me faithful, putting me into the ministry; Who was before a blasphemer, and a persecutor, and injurious: but I obtained **mercy**, because I did it ignorantly in unbelief. And the grace of our Lord was exceeding abundant with faith and love which is in Christ Jesus. This is a faithful saying, and worthy of all acceptation, that Christ Jesus came into the world to save sinners; of whom I am chief. Howbeit for this cause I obtained **mercy**, that in me first Jesus Christ might shew forth all longsuffering, for a pattern to them which should hereafter believe on him to life everlasting.*
1 Timothy 1:12-16 (Emphases mine)

Paul dubbed himself chief among sinners. That's because our paths never crossed. Good thing he would never know me until we meet in heaven. And even then, the joy of spending glorious eternity together with the Lord would drown any memory of the mistakes and the sins we both made or committed.

My life wasn't any better than that of Paul or any of the thieves on the crosses. I was an ignorant, clueless, wretched, and miserable sinner. Sure, I'd heard the gospel before, as a student both in high school and university. I knew the truth. I just didn't feel okay with that "boring lifestyle." I wanted to live holy, but not at the expense of "enjoying" my life. Looking back on those years, I can't stop thanking God for His mercy that spared my life, and made it possible for me to tell of His goodness.

For all have sinned, and come short of the glory of God.
Romans 3:23

I was numbered with the "all." But through the death of Jesus on the cross, I received God's mercy in place of judgment. The saved thief received it while hanging on his cross. And because it never waxes old, the same mercy is available to as many as surrender their lives to Jesus, repent of their sins, and pick up their crosses to follow Him.

Salvation overtook condemnation

Of all forms of punishment for crimes during the Roman Empire, crucifixion was considered the worst, reserved solely for vilest offenders. Once a criminal was nailed to the cross, there was no escape. Within hours, his condemnation would follow him to his afterlife.

But on one glorious day, a new record was set. A thief had been sentenced to death by crucifixion. If he had attorneys, they were unable to save his life. And since he was already nailed to the cross, it was over, it was done, and his fate was sealed. Drops of blood plopping with every gasp for breath signaled that the slow but sure death process had kicked in, marking the end of the road for him.

Suddenly, something nudged him to turn to the Man in the middle and do so within the short time he had left. He realized that, though man could not save him from man's temporary punishment, the Man on the middle cross could save him from God's eternal punishment. Without thinking *how* or *what if,* he asked Jesus to remember him in His kingdom. Remember him? That could mean different things.

. . . *When you get to your kingdom, remember to pray that I don't feel the heat of hell fire.*

. . . *I know I'm going to hell. But please when you get to your kingdom, remember to come pull me out of the fire.*

I doubt if he knew the meaning of that sentence, or if he knew that the Man had a kingdom beyond this earth. But without further ado, he asked and Jesus granted his request. And right there on the cross, salvation overtook condemnation. Now because of Christ's death on the cross, any sinner who repents of his (her) sins will receive salvation in place of condemnation. Guaranteed.

Foye Adedokun

Bondage gave way to freedom

There are various kinds of bondage. Some people are in bondage of poverty. Like generations before them, they carry a yoke of poverty around. No matter how hard they work, their condition remains the same and they don't know why. On the other hand, some people are in bondage to wealth. They're super rich. The things they can't buy are things they don't want, or things not sold. But their wealth is all they think of, so much so it deprives them of good sleep. No wonder Solomon prayed that God should give him neither poverty nor riches (Proverbs 30:8).

I used to think that was a stupid prayer. I can understand not wanting to be poor. But what's wrong with being stinking rich and living in grandeur? Well, I perfectly understand it now. Both extremes can sever your relationship with God because one holds as much rule over your heart as the other. Poverty will make you doubt God by controlling your thoughts; and riches can get you pompous against God by controlling your emotions. That means you're a slave to either one. And that goes for anything that you allow to rule over you (Matthew 6:21; Romans 6:16).

There's human bondage, the kind that the children of Israel suffered in Egypt under king Pharaoh. It was an oppressive and enslaving bondage that kept them bound for over four centuries.

However, the worst form of bondage in this life is bondage to sin. To be in bondage of sin is to be under the dictatorship of

114

Satan, the worst taskmaster of any soul. Every aspect of such life is miserable. There's no peace, no joy, no satisfaction. Each day is filled with sadness and constant apprehension. How I wish the repentant thief gave a short documentary of his life before he died. I bet he lived in perpetual fear of getting caught—at night, during the day, everywhere, every time.

Verily, verily, I say unto you, Whosoever committeth sin is the servant of sin.
John 8:38

Up until that moment when he turned to the Savior, that thief was in bondage of sin. But thank God for Jesus, and for the cross. Before his life ended, his bondage gave way to freedom. Because of the shed blood of Christ, any sinner can go before the Lord and ask to be liberated from the bondage of sin, just like the thief did on the cross. The liberation that he received is the same that many sinners have been receiving ever since, myself included.

Unless you secure that freedom, your life is heading in a destructive direction. Maybe your sins were committed in secret and it's not that you don't want to repent, you just don't want to be exposed. Let me remind you that Satan could be using that fear trick to prevent you from repenting, so he can have the final victory over your soul. If he can get you to think that your sins are the worst, he sure got you. But remember that if you successfully hide your sins now, you cannot hide them forever because, at the judgment throne, all sinners will be exposed.

Do you desire to be free? Then I've got good news for you. All you have to do is repent of your sins, confess them, pick up your cross, and follow Jesus. And that freedom will be yours, now and through eternity. Aren't you glad it's that simple?

Shame and ridicule led to fame and righteousness

For years in my country, many of the criminals that were sentenced to death were executed by firing squad in public places, like an open field or the beach. But from the last few years, any death sentence criminal is driven to his hometown and executed in front of his family house. Just think of the shame and ridicule the family will have to live with for a long time.

There are varying accounts of Christ's crucifixion. Every artist's impression that I've seen of Christ on the cross shows Him with a piece of cloth around His loins, suggesting some residual sense of decency in His murderers. Other accounts discredit that as a cover-up of the original scene, asserting that He was, indeed, crucified bare-naked. Considering His killers' proclivity for evil, I'm more inclined to believe the latter than I would the former. But whereas the latter claim remains only theoretically plausible, one fact remains inarguably valid: That what happened on that day on Golgotha was no fun picnic or parade of splendor. It was a disgraceful scene.

116

The main purpose of execution in any society is not only to discourage others from committing crimes, but also to shame and ridicule the offenders. For the two thieves crucified alongside Jesus, I say that notion was terrific. But for Jesus, that notion was terrible. I wonder what those religious leaders intended to achieve with such flagrant and vindictive attitude toward a Man with an inimitable record of good deeds. He raised the dead, restored sight to the blind, made the deaf to hear, made the dumb to speak, and healed all manner of sickness and disease. He helped all and hurt none. And that was a good excuse to shame and ridicule Him?

Thank God they failed and their purpose didn't materialize. Just three days later, pathetic liars became sore losers, when the Man they thought they had successfully murdered rose from the soldier-guarded grave—victorious, alive, and heralded by the rapture of sleeping saints, who barely waited for Him to arise before flying out of their quake-opened tombs (Matthew 27:51-52).

Over two thousand years after that day, the gospel move remains unstoppable, as generations of souls from oceans beyond Golgotha, are boldly and unashamedly drawn to the One that the dogmatists nailed to the cross of shame and ridicule. In the long run, their crucifixion plan to shame and ridicule Christ only fueled the flames of His fame and righteousness. Halleluyah!!!

Love conquered hatred

Horrendous is an understatement to describe the attitude of the religious leaders toward Jesus. Everything about Him gave them a frenzy of hateful emotions that they seemed to enjoy.

They disputed His virgin birth.

They attacked His humanity.

They blasphemed His identity.

They doubted His authenticity.

They resented His preaching.

They spited His teachings.

They opposed His views.

They rejected His divinity.

They demonized His power.

They ridiculed His miracles.

They questioned His authority.

They slammed His audacity.

They slandered His Messiahship.

They relegated His status.

They detested His personality.

They mocked His appearance.

They despised His fame.

They loathed His Name.

They persecuted His followers.

They abused His humility.

They victimized His vulnerability.

They plotted His death, "purchased" Him like a slave, and laid charges against Him, all false.

He was received like an enemy, portrayed as a liar, accused of insurrection, treated like an impostor, arrested like a traitor, dragged like a thug, paraded like a thief, pilloried like a murderer, scourged like a prisoner, mutilated like a sacrificial lamb, tried like a felon, sentenced like a convict, and executed like a criminal. They even "parted His garments, casting lots" for them (Matthew 27:35).

And had they not seen Him in person, they would have denied all accounts of His existence as mere phantasms playing out as realistic beliefs in the minds of misinformed followers. The only thing the religious bigots embraced about Jesus was their passionate hatred for Him. They hated to love Him as much as they loved to hate Him because His teachings were against what they believed and practiced, and that to them was a moral abomination.

Those cantankerous fanatics thrived on principles that were morally skewed and left no room to embrace anyone not in their ring or on their side. Nobody could question their customs and values because they believed they were always right. If it was their norm, then it was normal. But they failed to realize that, just because something is the norm doesn't mean it's normal or right.

Sadly, what happened then still happens today, having to

deal with people who are filled with inexplicable hatred toward other people. In fact, some folks are gratified by hatred. They vent on other people on grounds of any form of differences—lifestyle, cultural, and especially, religious differences. Like Paul before his conversion, they're insensitively avowed to inflicting pain of any degree on those not in their group.

Otherwise, what justification can anyone give for burning people alive, drowning people in acid, or beheading people? Would it be morally, religiously, or spiritually legit to use God as the justifying defense of such atrocities? Far from it. The God that I know and serve is a God of love.

When these workers of iniquity claim that they love God, I wonder if they're talking about the living God of heaven or an inanimate object that they carved out of something. If they truly think they're doing all that evil as service to God, then I question the source of their knowledge and the validity of their claim. I don't know what their holy books say, but this is what my Bible says.

Beloved, let us love one another: for love is of God; and every one that loveth is born of God, and knoweth God. He that loveth not knoweth not God; for God is love. Beloved, if God so loved us, we ought also to love one another. God is love; and he that dwelleth in love dwelleth in God, and God in him.
1 John 4:7-8, 11, 16

If you truly love God, then you have to love the people He created. He not only commands love, He demonstrated it. With the death of His Son, He proved that Golgotha hatred was no match for Calvary love, for right there on the cross, God's love conquered man's hatred.

Those who act contrary to love are enemies of God, agents of evil, and disciples of Satan. In the sight of God, their religious services are abominations, baseless and useless.

Jesus died for all sinners. He died for you. He died for me. He died for the hands nailing Him and the mouths mocking Him. As they crucified Him, they thought they had won. But they failed to realize that they could only kill His body, they could not kill His love for humanity. He loves sinners, He loves saints. He loves the unloving, and even, the unlovable.

In everything you do, let love prevail. Love others the way you want others to love you. Don't treat anybody the way you don't want anybody to treat you. If your religion permits you to be wicked and hateful toward other people, I suggest you reconsider your stand with the ultimate Judge of the universe. You can't claim to be His servant and be using His Holy Name to perpetrate your evil agenda against His creation.

And for us Christians, to profess Christ and not love as He loves, amounts to embracing the cross without embracing the love it epitomizes, and the love of the Savior who died on it.

Endless hope derailed hopeless end

What a pity. Those two thieves had lived rough lives. They made others cry just so they could laugh. There had to be better options than that insane path they followed. Now, they were on the last laps of their miserable lives, which would soon end in a most hopeless manner. After all, what hope could there be for a doomed criminal that was already nailed to the cross?

Hmm, wonders, they say, shall never end. To think that a criminal, who was only hours—or minutes—away from taking his last breath to hell, could still make heaven and spend eternity with Jesus. Incredibly wonderful. That exactly is what the cross is all about. It's the place where victims of hopelessness run to and receive hope.

When the saved thief asked Jesus to remember him in His kingdom, he did so as a hopeless sinner. On this side of life, he was a hopeless nutcase. Society had written him off. The law of man had convicted him. The court of man had sentenced him to death. The hands of men had nailed him to the cross and it was over for him. Well, as far as his earthly journey was concerned, that was all true. But once he turned to the Savior, a hopeless end became an endless hope, all in the blink of an eye.

His death on the cross brought his earthly journey to an end. But on the other side, he would open his eyes to a host of gathered saints, extending their angelic hands of fellowship to usher him home to paradise. What a glorious heavenly welcome that would be for a notorious earthly criminal.

Like that thief, I was a spiritual vagabond on a journey to a hopeless end. As a steadfast member of the choir, a Sunday school teacher, a punctual churchgoer and one who paid inaccurate tithes when she felt like, how could anyone convince me that I wasn't saved? To the best of my knowledge, I was good enough for heaven. Oh how I thank God that I didn't die in my ignorance, that I was redeemed from the path of destruction before it was too late.

When Jesus hung on the cross, He had me in mind. He never forced me to accept Him. But when I did, He never rejected me. He set me free from sin and gave me an endless hope to spend eternity with Him. I may not be nailed to a wooden cross by the hands of men. But I willfully cling to it in my heart because it was on it that my Savior shed His blood for me. Through His pain and agony, He secured me peace and harmony with God.

What hopeless situation are you in right now? Everything looks gloomy, with no end in sight. I suggest you take it to the foot of the cross and lay it down there. Then watch God turn everything around for His own glory. But more important than your situation is your salvation. Are you saved? If Christ returns today, or if you die today, what will your fate be in eternity? Give your life to Jesus, so you too can secure an endless hope in paradise.

4

The Christ

For as through the one man's disobedience many were made
sinners, even so through the obedience of the one, many will be
made righteous. That as sin reigned in death, even so grace might
reign through righteousness to eternal life through Jesus Christ
our Lord.
Romans 5:19, 21, WEB

A long time ago, I contracted a deadly disease from my parents, which they contracted from their own parents. The disease was passed down from generations back. And since my parents didn't know that they had the disease, they had no idea that I was infected, right from the day of conception. As a baby, nothing on the outside indicated anything negative. After all, I was only an innocent little child.

For years growing up, I lived with this deadly disease that I knew nothing about. Though a silent killer, it dwarfs any disease known to man. The symptoms are masked, known and apparent only to those who have been through it, and have been healed of it. Sadly, countless folks are dying with it either because they ignore its warning signs, they're too proud to admit its existence in their

124

lives, or they don't realize they have it. It's easy to seek help when there's a need. But what happens when you don't know you need help? By now, you probably know the disease I had. It's called cancer of the soul, the most common form of cancer contracted through natural conception—fertilization of the egg by sperm (Psalm 51:5). To be born with it is not as catastrophic as dying with it. But how do I know if I have this disease? Good question.

Being filled with all unrighteousness, sexual immorality, wickedness, covetousness, malice; full of envy, murder, strife, deceit, evil habits, secret slanderers, backbiters, hateful to God, insolent, haughty, boastful, inventors of evil things, disobedient to parents, without understanding, covenant breakers, without natural affection, unforgiving, unmerciful; who, knowing the ordinance of God, that those who practice such things are worthy of death, not only do the same, but also approve of those who practice them.
Romans 1:29-32, WEB

Now the deeds of the flesh are obvious, which are: adultery, sexual immorality, uncleanness, lustfulness, idolatry, sorcery, hatred, strife, jealousies, outbursts of anger, rivalries, divisions, heresies, envy, murders, drunkenness, orgies, and things like these; of which I forewarn you, even as I also forewarned you, that those who practice such things will not inherit God's Kingdom.
Galatians 5:19-21, WEB

But for the cowardly, unbelieving, sinners, abominable, murderers, sexually immoral, sorcerers, idolaters, and all liars, their part is in the lake that burns with fire and sulfur, which is the second death.
Revelation 21:8, WEB

125

A person may die of a natural disease and make heaven. But to die of unrepented sins is a direct journey to hell. If you notice any of the listed symptoms in your life, please seek help immediately, just like I did when I noticed some of them in my life. Through prompt and proper medical care, a person may be cured of cancer, and indeed, all manner of disease. For cancer of the soul, the only cure is blood transfusion from a Universal Donor called Jesus.

But how did His blood become the only cure for sins? Well, it all happened over two thousand years ago, when a virgin named Mary received a divine visitation from an angel.

Now in the sixth month, the angel Gabriel was sent from God to a city of Galilee, named Nazareth, to a virgin pledged to be married to a man whose name was Joseph, of David's house. The virgin's name was Mary. Having come in, the angel said to her, "Rejoice, you highly favored one! The Lord is with you. Blessed are you among women!" . . . Behold, you will conceive in your womb, and give birth to a son, and will call his name 'Jesus.'
Luke 1:26-31, WEB

According to the words of the angel, Jesus was born, not just for the sake of being born, but to die and shed His blood as atonement for our sins (1 John 2:1-2). Thirty-three years after His birth, that purpose was perfected.

One day on Golgotha, Jesus was crucified by brainwashed religious leaders, whose malevolent attitude was second only to

126

their non-admission of guilt for any wrongdoing. Their willingness to hammer nails into the veins of a fellow human being was a great proof of their evil hearts and their deep ignorance about the things of the kingdom. They thought they were doing God a service by getting rid of the miracle worker, who "not only had broken the sabbath" (John 5:18), but also "thought it not robbery to be equal with God" (Philippians 2:6). Little did they know that a divine purpose was being fulfilled. Like a sheep gone astray, humanity was lost and without direction. But He, "the Son of Man came to seek and to save that which was lost" (Luke 19:10).

He didn't have to come to this world in human form, but He did so He can relate to our feelings and pains. He didn't have to die, but He did so we can live. For all to come to repentance, He paid the ultimate price with His life. And as He bled for my sins and yours, He made seven statements between the time He was nailed to the cross and the time He died, each one a profound message to the world.

1st Statement:

Father, forgive them; for they know not what they do.

And when they were come to the place, which is called Calvary, there they crucified him, and the malefactors, one on the right hand, and the other on the left. Then said Jesus, Father, forgive them; for they know not what they do. And they parted his raiment, and cast lots.
Luke 23:33-34

According to Luke, Christ's first statement from the cross was a prayer asking His Father, God, to forgive His killers. It's of no use wondering why He would pray such prayer for people who crucified Him for the sins He didn't commit. He was treated with great animus—lied against, slapped, mocked, spat on, beaten, bruised, stripped naked, pushed, dragged, ridiculed, sentenced to death, nailed to the cross, and crucified by order of an adversarial judicial system of many evil opponents against one innocent Man. Justice swapped places with injustice as Barabbas, a condemned murderer and insurrectionist, was commuted of his death sentence and released, while my Savior was convicted of nothing and yet, scourged and sentenced to death by crucifixion (Mark 15:7-15).

Hanging there on the cross, in pain, in agony, thirsty, sweating, bleeding, and exhausted, He prayed for His assailants. "Father, forgive them; for they know not what they do." *Really, Jesus? Really? C'mon bruh, those killers knew exactly what they were doing. They were murdering you, don't you get it? They were neither blind nor stupid to nail their bully comrades or their own fast-hammering hands to the cross. Don't tell me they don't know what they were doing.* Settled. Now, let's consider the different facets of that prayer.

One, it was an offer of forgiveness by reason of ignorance. And I should be somersaulting right now because, according to Jesus, the reason I lived a sinful life was because I didn't know what I was doing.

- The reason those two thieves led criminal lives was because they didn't know what they were doing.

- The reason Judas betrayed Him was because he didn't know what he was doing.

- The reason Pilate took side with the crowd to crucify Him was because he didn't know what he was doing.

- The reason Peter denied Him three times was because he didn't know what he was doing.

- The reason His disciples fled and deserted Him was because they didn't know what they were doing.

- The reason Paul persecuted His followers was because he didn't know what he was doing.

- The reason people behead, burn alive, and shoot other people is because they don't know what they're doing.

In that case, since Christ already prayed for our forgiveness, all sinners should go to heaven because obviously, no sinner knows what he (she) is doing. So how come some sinners are saved and others are not? I'm glad you asked, and the answer is repentance.

Christ's prayer of forgiveness from the cross held true for sinners back then, including His killers, and still holds true for ALL sinners today, tomorrow, and evermore, till His return to earth. But, for it to be truly effective, the sinner must repent of his (her) sins and accept Jesus as Lord and Savior. The penitent thief did, Paul did, Peter did, and I did. If the other thief had repented and asked for forgiveness, he too would have received the promise of paradise. If the saved thief did not repent and he died a sinner, he would have gone to hell fire.

A father prays for his children to score good grades and be great in life. That prayer will avail for the child that studies well and works toward becoming great. For the child who doesn't care, the prayer is futile and of no effect, and no claim of ignorance can change the situation. That's how it is with salvation.

I know that logic has no place in salvation, and neither does human judgment. But I also know that Jesus' prayer on the cross gives no impunity from the consequences of sin. Ignorance of the law is no excuse to break the law. If you die a sinner, a claim of ignorance won't save you from eternal damnation. The Bible says, "My people are destroyed for lack of knowledge" (Hosea 4:6). If you douse yourself with gasoline and set yourself on fire, claim as much ignorance as you wish, it won't prevent you from burning.

Your lack of spiritual knowledge may make it difficult for you to grasp the seriousness of the eternal repercussion of your sinful actions. But that doesn't mean you don't know that your actions are evil.

And this is the condemnation, that light is come into the world, and men loved darkness rather than light, because their deeds were evil.
John 3:19

A thief may not know how dire the consequences will be if caught, but he still hides from the law because he knows his actions are evil.

Two, spiritually speaking, we can say that the killers of Jesus didn't know what they were doing, in the sense that they were being used to fulfill the prophecy spoken about Him years before that day.

For dogs have surrounded me. A company of evildoers have enclosed me. They have pierced my hands and feet.
Psalm 22:16

As "a company of evildoers," they were ignorant of His divinity and the atoning power of the blood they were shedding. But they definitely knew they were killing a person with feelings like them. And I know without a doubt that none of them would want to die the same way. Yet, if any of them repented and asked for forgiveness, he would be forgiven.

131

And the same goes for you and I. Every sin we committed, or may commit, is considered an act of ignorance. But we still have to confess them and ask for forgiveness before we can be forgiven.

Three, it's a prayer of unconditional forgiveness.

And forgive us our debts, as we forgive our debtors. For if ye forgive men their trespasses, your heavenly Father will also forgive you: But if ye forgive not men their trespasses, neither will your Father forgive your trespasses.
Matthew 6:12, 14-15

And forgive us our sins; for we also forgive every one that is indebted to us.
Luke 11:4

As they nailed, He prayed.

• How easy is it to pray for someone inflicting pain on you while he appears to be enjoying it?

• How easy is it to pray for someone who douses you with gasoline and sets you on fire?

• How easy is it to pray for someone who's about to behead you?

• How easy is it to pray for someone who took the life of your loved one?

• How easy is it to pray for people who grab you like a chicken and toss you inside a den of lions?

• How easy is it to pray for people that are hauling stones on your head?

• How easy is it to pray for someone whose flagrant lies put you

behind bars for years, or send you to the death row, for an offense you didn't commit?

Let's be honest, it's not easy praying for them, much less forgiving them. And yet, Jesus did exactly that to teach us that forgiveness leaves no room for options. With that simple prayer, He practicalized what He preached, and demonstrated what He taught. Forgiveness may be difficult, but it's not impossible.

In Acts, a group of evil men revolted against Stephen, whom God gave "the power to work great miracles and wonders among the people" (Acts 6:8). He was falsely accused of saying "terrible things against Moses and God!" (6:11). Not long after, he was arrested. Through the power of the Holy Spirit, Stephen gave an impassioned speech, which only made matters worse for him. As he declared his vision of heaven and of seeing Jesus standing beside God, he was attacked, dragged out, and stoned to death. But as the stones landed on him, "he kneeled down, and cried with a loud voice, Lord, lay not this sin to their charge" (Acts 7:60). He was asking God to forgive those who were stoning him.

Close your eyes and picture yourself in that situation. I don't think it was easy for him, but he did it anyway. By praying that prayer, he wasn't setting them free from the consequences of their actions. Rather, he was freeing his own mind of unforgiveness.

When you pray for your enemies as instructed by Christ, you not only free your heart of any bitterness against them, but you also set yourself free from all hindrances to your prayers and your eternity with Jesus. That doesn't mean that those who do evil against you will go free. Your prayer doesn't free them from God's judgment and punishment.

Like those who crucified Jesus and those who stoned Stephen to death, your enemies must repent of their sins and ask God for forgiveness before they can be forgiven. But on your own part, do what you should do and leave the judgment to God.

2nd Statement:

Verily I say unto thee, Today shalt thou be with me in paradise.

And one of the malefactors which were hanged railed on him, saying, If thou be Christ, save thyself and us. But the other answering rebuked him, saying, Dost not thou fear God, seeing thou art in the same condemnation? And we indeed justly; for we receive the due reward of our deeds: but this man hath done nothing amiss. And he said unto Jesus, Lord, remember me when thou comest into thy kingdom. And Jesus said unto him, Verily I say unto thee, Today shalt thou be with me in paradise.
Luke 23:39-43

To those who have never been here, America is paradise. In a desperate attempt to come here, people risk their precious lives just to step on the "streets of gold." Many drown crossing oceans by boat, or perish in the desert after walking days in a real "dry and weary land, where there is no water" or food. And many are shot dead by border guards while trying to jump the walls over to "paradise." Except being born into poor countries, those folks did nothing to warrant the hardship they suffer. For them, making ends meet is a challenge, a life-long misfortune that leaves them with no options but to seek livelihood elsewhere.

Sadly, when or if they make it here, they realize that the paradise they look forward to isn't so paradisiacal as they envisage. The streets are not gold and the country has her own challenges. If you don't possess the legal documents to live here, then you're in for real trouble. Obtaining those documents may take anywhere between few years and forever. And even more, the applicant must have a clean record, with no history of crime, before he (she) can be approved.

But one day in Damascus, on a hill called Golgotha, a criminal was granted instant visa to the heavenly country with real streets of gold. Under the law, the fact that he was a criminal should have made it impossible for him to obtain entry into heaven. That guy made a vocation out of crime. And if laurels were available for criminal achievements, he and the other fella would have won them uncontested. They lived by crime and therefore, deserved to die for it and go straight to hell.

If "the wages of sin is death" (Romans 6:23), then no one who has ever sinned should make heaven. That's correct. But as much as the law of man may want a person to remain in bondage, the love of God sets us free from bondage through His Son Jesus Christ.

The law of man crucified the penitent thief for his crimes. He received wages that were commensurate with his offense, and he died the physical death. But by asking Jesus to remember him in His kingdom, and sincerely so, the love of God set him free from the wages of everlasting punishment in hell fire. Can be it any easier? Can it be any freer? Can it be any more readily available? I don't think so.

Personally, I envy that thief. He earned his salvation the

easiest way possible, and never had to worry about all the post-salvation requirements. I don't even know how to describe his case. Was he crucified with Jesus by accident, coincidence, luck, or destiny? Whatever moved him to make that request, couldn't the same thing have moved the other thief? Should we call it a "doctrine of election," which is the belief that some people are predestined to go to heaven regardless of their sins? Or, was it a case of "Jacob have I loved, but Esau have I hated" (Romans 9:13), making it appear like he was God-picked to be saved on the cross on that day?

Maybe it's quite irrelevant to ask questions because really, that's not as important as the good news in that short story of unmerited favor: That Christ spoke those words, not only to the thief, but to every unsaved person who is willing to forsake the way of sin and accept Him as Lord and Savior. It's that simple. I'm glad the promise of paradise didn't end with that thief. I've turned my life over to Jesus. And I know that as long as I remain in His love, I too will spend eternity with Him.

If you turn to Him and **genuinely** ask Him to remember you in His kingdom, He will give you the same reverberating answer that He gave to the thief—*Today shalt thou be with me in paradise.* And for as long as you remain faithful to Him, the truth of the promise remains interminable, because God's promises in Christ are yes and amen (2 Corinthians 1:20); and once spoken,

Foye Adedokun

will not return unto Him void (Isaiah 55:11).

Jesus says, "All that the Father giveth me shall come to me; and him that cometh to me I will in no wise cast out" (John 6:37). If you come to Him or call on Him, He won't cast you out. I look forward to seeing you in paradise.

3rd Statement:

Woman, behold thy son! Then saith he to the disciple, Behold thy mother!

Now there stood by the cross of Jesus his mother, and his mother's sister, Mary the wife of Cleophas, and Mary Magdalene. When Jesus therefore saw his mother, and the disciple standing by, whom he loved, he saith unto his mother, Woman, behold thy son! Then saith he to the disciple, Behold thy mother! And from that hour that disciple took her unto his own home.
John 19:25-27

More often than not, a dying parent is surrounded by the children, grandchildren, and, great-grandchildren, if any. Extended family members can be present too. It's a sign of affection for the departing. The other side of that is when parents bury their own child, a bitter, sad, sorrowful, and life-altering experience that no parents should ever go through. And that's the more reason why Mary, the mother of Jesus, never ceases to amaze me.

As a mother, I know I can't stand and watch anyone hit my child with anything. Chances are Mary saw Jesus whipped, pushed, dragged, and spat upon. She watched helplessly as He staggered when forced to carry His cross with His already fatigued and terribly lacerated body. And from the above passage, we know that she was on Golgotha, watching and weeping as the inches-long nails were hammered into her Son's hands and feet, and the cross got covered with her Son's gushing blood. That she even went as far as standing at the foot of the cross (John 19:25) makes it highly probable that the clothes she wore to Golgotha were red-stained by her Son's splattered blood, a souvenir of her greatest sorrow.

I wonder how she could stand through all that, because honestly, I would have passed out. Perhaps she was waiting for the moment when her Son would disappear and everything would be over, a moment of a lifetime that she wouldn't want to miss. But alas, her Son didn't disappear. He endured the crucifixion, so He could perfect the work of redemption for which she delivered Him thirty-three years earlier.

When she gave birth to Jesus, the Bible tells us that many things happened, "But Mary kept all these things, and pondered them in her heart" (Luke 2:19). No idea how many such things she kept to herself. She probably knew that her first-born child would be different. But I doubt if it ever crossed her mind that things would get that nightmarish.

Now standing by the cross, her Son, though in monumental agony, saw her and was moved with love and compassion for her. It wasn't because Mary had no other children (Matthew 13:55-56). But as the first Child and first Son, Jesus knew He held a special place, both in the family and in His mother's aching heart. And He wanted to make sure she was in good hands after He was gone.

The Bible didn't give the exact identity of the person Jesus picked to care for His mother. But since it was the disciple whom

Jesus loved, we can safely assume it was John (John 21:20-24).

But why not pick one of His own blood brothers instead of a disciple? Well, it all goes back to the Lord doing His things His way. He knew what no one else in that crowd knew. And there must be a reason why He chose John, a reason we will never know until we get to heaven. But there are lessons to learn from that special move of care and affection toward His mother.

One, that in our pain and suffering, we must be cognizant of those who are there for us, with us, and determined not to leave our side. Life sometimes takes an unexpected turn for the worse and we find ourselves in a situation against our wish. During that difficult time, some people will stick with us when others flee. If there's anything we can do to let such people know how much we trust them, and how greatly we appreciate their kindness, let's endeavor to do it.

John stood by Jesus through His most difficult moment. That tells a great deal about his character and explains why he was the disciple Jesus loved. And to let John know how much He appreciated and trusted him as a disciple, Jesus committed the most important person in His life—His mother—to his care.

Two, that you shouldn't assume that things will automatically fall into place when you're gone. Whatever you can do for anyone, especially your parent, do it while you're alive. Jesus loved John and He knew John would do a good job caring for Mary, like he would his own mother. He apparently saw in him what no one else saw—a caring spirit. Who knows the kind of people Mary's other children were? There's no mention of their presence on Golgotha. But John was there.

All the same, Jesus didn't assume John would instinctively take Mary home after He was gone. He took care of business while He was still alive. Don't second-guess what may happen once you're gone. Just because people are nice to you now doesn't mean they'll be nice to your people when you're dead. Take care of business while you have the means and life to do so.

Three, that nobody prays or wishes for the death of a loved one. But for reasons we may never understand, it happens and leaves us devastated. And there's nothing we can do about it. When Jesus made that statement to His mother, He was lovingly asking her to move on with her life. His death was inevitable and there was **nothing** she could do about it. So, it was better for her to accept the reality of Him being gone, and get used to John filling in the vacuum.

I know it can be tough coping with the loss of a loved one, especially a wonderful child. If you have lost a loved one, please accept my condolences. I sincerely pray that God will grant you the fortitude to bear the loss. And I pray that the balm of Gilead be sent from heaven to heal your aching heart. But please ask the Lord for the grace to move on and don't tie yourself down to the past that you can neither change nor regain.

God says He'll give us beauty for ashes (Isaiah 61:3). The problem is, when He approaches us with His beauty, He finds us holding tight and refusing to let go of our ashes—of sorrow, disappointment, and failure. God wants the best for us, but it's up to us to receive it or reject it. Had Mary refused to follow John home, she would have missed out on the blessing of a good life after a terrible tragedy.

> To receive God's promise of beauty, unclench your tight fists and let go of the ashes.

Please don't let your sorrow keep you from enjoying the blessings God has in store for you. Accept His provision and bless His Name for it.

Four, that if you're in position to fill in the gap for anyone, don't hesitate, don't turn it down, and don't exploit it for selfish reasons.

I watched a movie about two men who were close friends and trusted each other to a confidential level. They both vowed that if anything happened to both husband and wife, and the children are underage, the living friend would take care of the deceased's children. To seal the deal, they added each other as signatories to their personal estates.

As fate had it, one of them died in a plane crash, along with his wife, leaving the orphaned children at the mercy of a trusted friend. Sadly, the supposedly trusted friend turned his back on the young children and denied them any access to their parents' fortune, leaving them in limbo of daily survival and any hope for the future.

From the moment Jesus spoke those words to John, the Bible says he "took her to his own home." That was a two-way trust. Jesus trusted that John would do a good job caring for His mother. And John proved trustworthy by doing exactly that after the death of His master.

Can anyone trust you that much? Do you care about the family of your deceased spouse, sibling, or friend, who all dearly loved you when they were alive? Remember that a caring spirit will heal a broken heart faster than a meal served on a golden plate with an awful attitude.

Five, that when we think no one is left, God will raise help from another source, and beyond our expectations.

Like I asked earlier, where were Mary's other children? Clearly, none of them cared enough to follow their mother or their brother to the cross. And if they did, they were not within sight, where they could be easily spotted. That wasn't surprising though because even His brothers didn't believe in Him (John 7:5). And most likely His sisters too didn't believe in Him. They were just as disappointing as the disciples that deserted Jesus.

But John not only followed Jesus to the cross, he stood where he could be seen, sticking his neck out at a most dangerous place and moment. He was a disciple who stood closer than a

144

brother. And whereas Mary thought her source of comfort was leaving, the Lord showed her another source of comfort, one that would love her like the One who would soon leave her.

Are you giving up on life because you feel you have come to the end of the road? Like Mary stood resilient till the end, refuse to leave the Lord's presence until He provides you the comfort you desire. Though things happening around you may make that seem like a wishful thinking or unrealistic fantasy, just hold on and don't give up because He has plans for you. He sees you and He feels your pain. And just when you think it's over, He says you're just starting. Trust Him and He will surely come through for you.

Six, that whenever God gives you an assignment, He will supply the life and means to complete it.

Of Jesus' twelve disciples, eleven were alive as at the time of His crucifixion. (Judas was already dead.) But of those eleven, do you know that only John lived to old age and died of natural causes? I'm not insinuating that the other ten died young and of unnatural causes because they were not chosen to care for Mary. But I'm categorically saying that, because John was given that assignment, his life was preserved so he could accomplish the task for which he was chosen.

When Moses fled Egypt after committing murder, he was forty years old (Exodus 2:12; Acts 7:23-30). When God sent him on the herculean mission to go and lead the Israelites out of Egypt, he "was fourscore years old" (Exodus 7:7). Why would God assign such a daunting task to an eighty-year-old man? Then for forty wearisome years, Moses led "about **six hundred thousand** on foot that were men, beside children. And a mixed multitude went up also with them; and flocks, and herds, even very much cattle" (Exodus 12:37-38, emphasis mine). When God relieved him of the task, he was one hundred and twenty years old. And it wasn't because he was fatigued, feeble, or blind. "His eye was not dim, nor his strength gone" (Deuteronomy 34:7, WEB). You know that kind of strength and skill can only come from God.

When Christ sent out his disciples for evangelism, He asked them to "take nothing for their journey, save a staff only; no scrip, no bread, no money in their purse: But be shod with sandals; and not put on two coats. And he said unto them, In what place soever ye enter into an house, there abide till ye depart from that place" (Mark 6:8-10). They didn't have to worry about survival because God would take care of them.

God supplies the provision for every commission, and gives the ability for every responsibility. It is He who works in us "both to will and to do of his good pleasure" (Philippians 2:13). Once Jesus told John to care for Mary, he took her home without asking questions or scratching his head, wondering how he would be able to do that. He knew that everything he would need to complete that task was already impliedly provided.

146

When He gives you an assignment or sends you on a mission, just make yourself available. He will make you able and supply everything you'll need to achieve His purpose—wisdom, strength, health, and all.

Seven, that every cloud of hopelessness has a silver lining of hope. At least once in a given lifetime, everyone experiences the moment when the heart's greatest hope seems so far away or totally lost, leaving us with shattered dreams and dashed expectations. And because we're spiritually myopic (1 Corinthians 13:12), directly or indirectly, our hopelessness clouds our vision and leaves us asking why and wondering how.

Can you imagine Mary's confusion as she watched her Son crucified? Which of her other children could love and take care of her the way Jesus did? What would those who knew her as the mother of the miracle-worker think? And if her Son would "reign over the house of Jacob for ever; and of his kingdom there shall be no end" (Luke 1:33), how would that come to pass after His death?

While she focused on her dying Son, she didn't realize that the disciple standing beside her would be the angel that would take care of her for the rest of her life. By asking His mother to behold John, Jesus was directly telling her to shift her focus from her cloud of sorrow and disappointment, and instead, to behold the silver lining of another wonderful son standing beside her. John was the silver lining of hope in Mary's cloud of hopelessness.

Foye Adedokun

We may not understand why God does what He does, and why He permits some things to happen. That's because our minds are too finite to comprehend the mind of an infinite God. But the Bible assures us that when we hope in God, we will not be put to shame (Romans 5:5), regardless of how hopeless our situation looks. As we pass through the dark tunnel, though the environment makes it impossible to deny the reality of fear, we must never let it render us blind to the light that God is shining at the end of the tunnel.

Satan will want you to see your situation as a cul-de-sac, a dead-end to nothing. But if you can hand it over to God, you'll be amazed at the new provision He has already prepared for you. And when that happens, accept and embrace it with gratitude, just like Mary accepted and embraced her new son, John, in place of her real Son, Jesus.

4th Statement:

Eli, Eli, lama sabachthani?

*Now from the sixth hour there was darkness over all the land unto
the ninth hour. And about the ninth hour Jesus cried with a loud
voice, saying, Eli, Eli, lama sabachthani? that is to say, My God,
my God, why hast thou forsaken me? Some of them that stood there,
when they heard that, said, This man calleth for Elias.*
Matthew 27:45-47

"My God, my God, why hast thou forsaken me?" It was a
cry of desperation, certainly embarrassing and grossly humiliating.
But coming from the Man who "said also that God was his father"
(John 5:18), how could that be?

A personal story of abandonment is better read or told, than
experienced. I've travelled that road before, the road of sorrow, of
anguish, of pain and suffering, caused by a father's abandonment
and forsakenness. Though I wasn't there at the cross, but reading
that cry from Christ brings back painful memories.

In real life, I suffered firsthand abandonment from my own
father, the man responsible for my birth. My father abandoned us
(my mother, my siblings, and myself) into an uncertain future,
where he left us like we never even existed. He discarded us like a
foul-smelling fart that needed to be released, so the body can have
some relief. Throwing us out of his life was a big relief to him.
Why would he care where we were sleeping when he didn't even
know if we were still living? We were not relevant.

149

To be abandoned by a loved one is a painful experience. It hurts and it creates a horrible feeling that the very person, in whose arms a child should feel the warm embrace of love and acceptance, is nowhere to be found when he (she) is desperately needed.

In the spiritual, it's easy to feel abandoned by God when things don't go the way we want. In my few years on earth, I've asked God so many whys than I can count. I hear myself asking why He lets this and that continue to happen despite my love for Him. Why is He not opening the windows of heaven despite my faithfulness in tithing and offering? After all, the covenant is two-sided (Malachi 3:10).

Once I fulfill my side of the covenant, I expect a reciprocal downpour of blessings in fulfillment of His side of the covenant. And when that doesn't happen, I get upset and demand an explanation, like He owes me one. But those moments don't necessarily represent my lack of faith in God. They're expressions of frustration borne out of disappointment.

When I think of my earthly father and think of my heavenly Father—God—I know without doubt that, whereas it was possible for my father to abandon me in my sufferings, the love that God has for me makes it impossible for Him to abandon me in any situation. As a mother, the love I have for my children makes it impossible for me to forget or abandon any of them. That reassures me that God can never abandon me because He cares about me more than I care about my children, or myself. Though situations and circumstances can make it appear like He doesn't care, nothing can be farther from the truth.

So, did God actually forsake Christ during His pain? NO!!! If God can't forsake me, how could He forsake His Only Son? The cry sure sounded like a cry of abandonment. But it wasn't because He was abandoned, but because His perfect humanity was active.

By tradition, a crown prince enjoys several royal privileges, just for being a crown prince living in the palace. He has servants to wait on him, chauffeurs to drive him places, cooks to prepare his meals, even bodyguards to follow him everywhere.

One day, the crown prince decides to go and live among some villagers, so he can use his princely power to help make their lives better. That means living like them, without any special favors and privileges, like Paul, who became everything to every man for the sake of the gospel (1 Corinthians 9:19-23). Sadly, the people the prince wants to help turn against him and subject him to unwarranted suffering. Like anyone else, he will feel the pain of bruising because he's human. But no amount of suffering imposed upon him can undo his royal princely title. Once a prince, forever a prince.

Jesus was perfectly divine before coming to earth. When He came to earth, He became perfectly human, but still fully endowed with His divine power.

In the beginning was the Word, and the Word was with God, and the Word was God. The same was in the beginning with God. And the Word was made flesh, and dwelt among us, (and we beheld his glory, the glory as of the only begotten of the Father,) full of grace and truth.
John 1:1-2, 14

While on earth, His humanity was brutalized by people who had no respect or any appreciation for His divinity. He felt real pain and agony on the cross, the same way He felt real sorrow and fatigue in the Garden of Gethsemane (Matthew 26:38; Luke 22:43). As He hung on the accursed and evil tree, laden with the sins of the whole world, God took His eyes off of Him, not because He forsook Him, but because His eyes are too pure to behold evil, or look on iniquity (Habakkuk 1:13).

I've had my fair share of painful experiences in life. But on the brighter side, I learned some unforgettable lessons from them.

• If I ask and don't receive, it's not because God has forsaken me or that He no longer cares about me.

• When answers to my prayers aren't as fast as I want or expect, it's not because God is slow. It's because I'm in a hurry.

• When I think He's too far away, He's right there beside me.

• When He seems so eerily silent, it's because I'm allowing my fears and worries to deafen me to His still small voice of assurance.

• And each time, what looks like the enemy's pursuit always turns out to be a push from God to get me to my victory.

As long as you remain in His love, you don't need to entertain feelings of abandonment. It doesn't mean you won't experience fear along the way. But He, the Shepherd of your soul, will be with you to the very end. God is God and will never cease to be God. He's never too fast and never late. He's perfect and always on time. He cares today, as much as He cared yesterday, and will care tomorrow.

Whatever you're going through, don't believe Satan's lie that God has forsaken you, forgotten you, or no longer cares about you. That it feels like it doesn't mean it is. Inasmuch as you're in His will, He "will never leave thee, nor forsake thee" (Hebrews 13:5).

5th Statement:

I thirst.

After this, Jesus knowing that all things were now accomplished,
that the scripture might be fulfilled, saith, I thirst.
John 19:28

Thirst is generally an indication of dry throat or a pressing need for water. But people also thirst for different things in life—fame, knowledge, promotion, achievement, approval, acceptance, money, wealth, love, better walk with God. However, one day on Calvary, the Savior of the world cried from the cross, "I thirst." And in His case, it was a cry for natural water to soothe His dry throat. But how was it possible that the Lord, Himself the living water, would be thirsty?

In His conversation with the Samaritan woman at Jacob's well, Jesus says, "Everyone who drinks of this water will thirst again, but whoever drinks of the water that I will give him will never thirst again; but the water that I will give him will become in him a well of water springing up to eternal life" (John 4:13-14, WEB).

As a well of living water, whoever drank or drinks of Him should never thirst again. So why was He thirsty? Did He suddenly dry up? No. But here again, as in His fourth statement, we see His perfect humanity at work. As He got closer to the completion of His mission, He became physically dehydrated and thirsty, having endured so much torture. I read that dying people express thirst while on their death bed. Should we then be surprised that our dying Savior expressed thirst while on His death cross? No. He was just being human.

Are you at that crossroad in life, where it feels like you have been drained of all energy? Unfortunately, the people you lean on to ease your pain only make it worse with words that feel like thorns in the flesh. Don't despair. Even Jesus in His agony cried out, "I thirst." But instead of water, they offered Him vinegar, a most degrading gesture toward a Man worthy of all honor in heaven and on earth. It can't be any worse than that.

6th Statement:

It is finished.

Now there was set a vessel full of vinegar: and they filled a spunge with vinegar, and put it upon hyssop, and put it to his mouth. When Jesus therefore had received the vinegar, he said, It is finished: and he bowed his head, and gave up the ghost.

John 19:29-30

It is finished can mean many things. It can mean the end of a task—a chore, an errand, or, an assignment. It can mean the completion of a race, an event, a challenge, or, a meeting. It can mean the accomplishment of a goal or a purpose. It can mean the end of cooperation, rivalry, agreement, or disagreement between opponents. It can mean termination of authority or stronghold that one party exploits to abuse the other, as it was during slavery. It can be used to express lack, therefore a need for more. And sadly, it can mean the end of life, when the soul exits the body.

When Jesus said, "It is finished" while still hanging on the cross, what exactly did He finish? Well, relative to Him, many things were finished. But to know what He finished, we need to know what He did. Going back to the beginning of His ministry, after His baptism in the Jordan River, His Father (God) endorsed Him with the descent of the Holy Spirit in a bodily shape like a dove, followed by His declaration, "Thou art my beloved Son; in thee I am well pleased" (Luke 3:22). The Bible puts His age at thirty years, the age He started His ministry (Luke 3:23).

Before going full-time, He retreated into the wilderness, where He spent forty days and forty nights in absolute fasting. After His fasting, Satan took a chance and attacked Him with three different temptations, each one marked by a woeful crushing of Satan's power by the Lord. But that was only the beginning of what He came to do.

And Jesus returned in the power of the Spirit into Galilee: . . . And he came to Nazareth, where he had been brought up: and, as his custom was, he went into the synagogue on the sabbath day, and stood up for to read. And there was delivered unto him the book of the prophet Esaias. And when he had opened the book, he found the place where it was written, The Spirit of the Lord is upon me, because he hath anointed me to **preach the gospel to the poor;** *he hath sent me to* **heal the brokenhearted,** *to* **preach deliverance to the captives,** *and* **recovering of sight to the blind,** *to* **set at liberty them that are bruised, To preach the acceptable year of the Lord.** *Luke 4:14-19* (Emphases mine)

In addition to other things, the above passage lists six major things that Jesus came to do.

1. Christ came to preach the gospel to the poor

In His sermon on the mount, Jesus says, "Blessed are the poor in spirit: for theirs is the kingdom of heaven" (Matthew 5:3). People pray and ask God for many things in this life. But I'm yet to meet one person who prays for poverty. Nobody wants to be poor because poverty produces sorrow. And if there's one thing a poor person wants more than anything else, it is to be rich. I know that because I've been there, lived it. However, that's not the type of poverty Jesus was talking about in that verse.

As physical poverty makes the poor sorrowful, spiritual poverty must produce sorrow in the heart of a spiritual destitute, pushing him (her) to seek knowledge.

By *the poor,* Jesus was inferring spiritual poverty, as it relates to lack of good knowledge about spiritual matters. Jesus came to earth to impart knowledge, so souls can be saved from destruction. Through His spoken words, billions of spiritually poor souls like me have gained immense spiritual wealth. And many, who would have perished in their sins, are restored and made worthy for the kingdom of heaven.

But, whereas a poor person can become rich through hard work or good job, it's only through the infallible Word of God that the poor in spirit can be made rich and ready for heaven. For that to be, Jesus came and preached the gospel to enlighten the weak understanding of those who are poor in the spirit.

2. Christ came to heal the brokenhearted

*But now, O LORD, thou art our father; we are the clay, and thou
our porter; and we all are the work of thy hand.*
Isaiah 64:8

The word *heal* suggests a wound or sickness, a physical
condition that can be treated with good medication and proper care.
But healing can also be used figuratively, relative to sorrow or
grief. So, how does that relate to a broken heart? Sorrow, of any
form and due to any reason, leads to a broken heart that only the
great Healer can mend. A human being is like pottery in the hands
of God. If a pot is broken, the potter puts it back together into one
whole piece, again. In the same way that only a potter can mend a
broken pottery, only the Lord can mend (heal) a broken heart.

Having lost everything he had in life, Job said, "My eye
also is dim by reason of sorrow. All my members are as a shadow"
(Job 17:7). At that point in his life, his sorrow was overwhelming
and monumental, too great for him to bear and too much for his
faith to handle. His heart was broken beyond mending by any
amount of comforting words coming from ordinary mortal man.
Any heart plagued by a sorrow of that magnitude would require
special healing from Jehovah Rapha—the Lord that healeth all
wounds—before it can be made whole again.

Are you entangled by a web of sorrows? Remember that
Christ came to heal the brokenhearted, to mend the heart shattered

by grief and anguish, to put back together the heart ripped apart by pain and tragedy, and to save the heart plagued by sorrow of sin. And since He also experienced sorrow (Mark 14:34), it's easy for Him to relate to the sorrow of those whose broken hearts He came to heal. Give Him a chance to do that for you.

3. Christ came to preach deliverance to the captives

Bondage has many facets. During Jesus' earthly ministry, many were bound by infirmities until they encountered Him.

• The two blind men, and one man who was unable to speak (Matthew 9).

• A man who was demonic, blind, and unable to speak (Matthew 12).

• The boy with epilepsy, who, on numerous occasions, had been thrown into fire and water (Matthew 17).

• Legion, the lunatic that lived among tombs, crying and cutting himself, and didn't even know it (Mark 5).

• The woman with twelve years issue of blood (Mark 5).

• The demon-possessed daughter of a Gentile woman (Mark 7).

• A man who was both deaf and dumb (Mark 7).

• Bartimaeus, a blind beggar (Mark 10).

• A paralytic that was brought to Jesus by four men (Luke 5).

• A woman who had been crippled and bent for eighteen years (Luke 13).

- A man with dropsy, a disease better known as edema (Luke 14).

- Ten lepers on the way to Jerusalem (Luke 17).

- The impotent man at the pool of Bethesda, who had been crippled in both legs for thirty-eight years (John 5).

- The man born blind (John 9).

- In addition, He also healed all manner of sickness and disease (Matthew 4:23).

Today, there are millions in prisons, incarcerated for crimes of varying degrees. And depending on the severity of the crime, jail time can be anywhere between few days to forever. Sadly, some are incarcerated for offenses they didn't commit, suffering unjustly every day. These are all examples of physical bondages.

But Jesus also came to set us free from the worst bondage, spiritual bondage—that of sin leading to eternal condemnation. In fact, the conversion of souls following His sermons and miracles was His main offense that led to His crucifixion (John 7:1, 31-32; 11:45-48; 12:9-13, 19). His Words opened the hearts of many, who, for the first time, realized their lack of knowledge of the truth, and admitted their ignorance.

Having been in darkness for so long, it was impossible for them not to appreciate light. They knew that the only way to avoid going to hell fire was to change and amend their ways. For them, that was very liberating because their spiritual blindfolds were removed, and they were able to discern between the lies of

161

the religious rulers and the truth that Jesus preached, taught, and demonstrated. That's the greatest deliverance any person can experience in life.

But how do we recognize spiritual bondage?

One, the presence of anything in your life that doesn't agree with the Word of God is evident of spiritual bondage (Galatians 5:19-21, Romans 21:8).

Two, anytime you feel a compulsive urge to do something that you won't do under normal circumstances, that's a spiritual bondage. Your spirit wants to stop, but your flesh is too weak. Each time you slip, you vow that'll be the last time. But before you know it, you find yourself doing it again. It can be anything from addiction to bad habits—gambling, smoking, partying, womanizing, overeating, idleness, staying out late, drunkenness, over-speeding, obsessive spending, pornography, spousal abuse, *et cetera*. You may think it's trivial. But something you consider trivial may be the very thing that will send you to your early grave, or even worse, to hell fire.

I pray you don't delay till it's too late for you. For that not to happen, give Jesus a chance in your life, so He can set you free. And if you're a believer, but still struggling with a compulsive urge to do things that you don't feel okay to do, then ask Jesus to help you overcome it.

Stand fast therefore in the liberty wherewith Christ hath made us
free, and be not entangled again with the yoke of bondage.
Galatians 5:1

Sin is enslaving and many are captivated by its insidious bait. Once trapped, they remain bound by its invisible fetters, completely unsuspecting of the eternal regret they're being led into. But no one encounters Christ and remains Satan's captive, because greater is our Savior who came to set us free from the bondage of sin, than Satan who walks about like a roaring lion, "seeking whom he may devour" (1 Peter 5:8).

Do yourself a favor. Allow Jesus to set you free before Satan devours you.

4. Christ came to preach recovery of sight to the blind

A blind person is someone without sight, either partially in one eye, or totally in both eyes. And whereas the partially blind may never require help to complete tasks, a totally blind person is mostly dependent on others for assistance with just about anything. I've seen quite a sight-full of blind people—from totally blind, to partially blind, to not blind at all but pretending to be.

But do you know it's possible to have perfect vision in both eyes and still be blind; and it's possible to be totally blind in both eyes and still have perfect vision? In the Bible, Jesus ministered healing to many that were physically blind. And they all received sight in their eyes. But when He talked about preaching recovery of sight to the blind, He was talking about spiritual blindness—the unregenerate souls, the blind at heart, the unbelievers, those who don't know Him, those who are spiritually lost because they won't accept Him as the only Way to heaven.

The most prominent cause of physical blindness is cataract. As physical cataract clouds the eye lens and makes it unable to see well, spiritual cataract clouds the heart and makes it unable to feel the need for a better understanding of the truth. And it can be any of the following:

a. Eternal security

Concept of eternal security teaches that once saved, forever saved because your sins after your salvation have no effect on your eternity with Christ, thus the liberty to sin without the fear of eternal retributions or earthly repercussions. That sounds more like a doctrine of eternal calamity than eternal security. And those who teach it and the people who believe it are all spiritually blind. If they read their Bibles, what do these verses mean to them?

But when the righteous turns away from his righteousness, and commits iniquity, and does according to all the abominations that the wicked man does, shall he live? None of his righteous deeds that he has done shall be remembered: in his trespass that he has trespassed, and in his sin that he has sinned, in them shall he die.
Ezekiel 18:24, WEB

When I tell the righteous, that he shall surely live; if he trust to his righteousness, and commit iniquity, none of his righteous deeds shall be remembered; but in his iniquity that he has committed, therein shall he die.
Ezekiel 33:13, WEB

Therefore let him who thinks he stands be careful that he doesn't fall.
1 Corinthians 10:12, WEB

From the above verses, it's very clear that it's possible to lose one's salvation.

In Jerusalem at the pool of Bethesda, Jesus healed a man who had been crippled for thirty-eight years. When Jesus later found him in the temple, He said to him, "Behold, you are made well. Sin no more, so that nothing worse happens to you" (John 5:1-14). Jesus was unequivocally telling him that if he went back into sins, a worse condition than his previous condition would come upon him.

Concept of eternal security is a killer doctrine and a hell-defying heresy. A person can forfeit his (her) salvation if such goes back to sin, and that person's life will take a turn for the worse. That was why Paul subjected his body to discipline, so he would not lose his salvation (1 Corinthians 9:27). If Paul did that, then every saved soul should do likewise.

That you're saved is no reason to commit sin. If you die in your sins, you will be judged as a sinner on the last day.

b. Programmed mindset

My mother raised all five of us, and church attendance was constant. At no time did she force us to go to church. But for her, church attendance was beyond passing interest, rain or sunshine, and we followed suit. That programmed mindset turned into a Sunday tradition with no spiritual returns to show for it.

I grew up religious, tongue-in-cheek. In my adult years, I taught children's Sunday school class. I joined the choir, I prayed, I fasted, I was baptized, I paid my "tithe" the way I deemed right. And I always had my Bible beside me when I slept. But, like many fake Christians, I was only a religious sinner, as far from the truth as the East is from the West. I was a stinking corpse in a dazzling angelic garment, and not a single fruit of the spirit in my life. Yet, nobody could convince me that I wasn't on track because I was blinded by my religious upbringing.

Were it not for Christ, I would have died as a sinner and gone to hell. Not because I wasn't religious, not because I didn't read or believe the Bible, not because I didn't know how to pray, not even because I didn't know about Jesus. But simply because, being all that actually blinded me and made salvation message sound like nothing more than what I already was and already knew.

I bless the Lord for setting me free from the chains of spiritual blindness.

c. Purgatory

Some people believe that if a person dies unsaved, the soul will go to Purgatory where it will undergo some form of cleansing to purge the individual of any traces of sin left in him (her) after death. For those that care about enjoying life before death, that sounds like a tantalizing excuse to ignore the gospel. If at all it's true, they obviously never care to ask about the intensity of the purging, what happens there, and how long it lasts. But I know it's not true, because the Bible says, "And as it is appointed unto men once to die, but after this the judgment" (Hebrews 9:27).

Don't be fooled into believing any heterodox teachings. Once you die, you're done. *C'est fini. Se terminó.* It's all over. Please refrain from any blind doctrine that will lead you to hell. If your spiritual leader chooses to stay blind, that's his life. But that's no excuse for you to live or stay blind. Don't let hell be the place where you will find out the truth.

d. Religious zeal

The religious leaders of Jesus' days had a special type of blindness—misdirected zeal. No doubt they were religious, maybe more than many believers of today. But if they loved God that much, why attack others who also loved Him, but in a different way? Their strict tenets and precepts gave them a malignant sense of entitlement that made them consider it a grave offense for anyone to either oppose or reject their beliefs and practices.

It was okay for them to be as religiously zealous as they wished. But those who were not part of them were forbidden from exercising any religious zeal, a hypocrisy sharply denounced by the Lord.

Woe unto you, scribes and Pharisees, hypocrites! for ye are like unto whited sepulchres, which indeed appear beautiful outward, but are within full of dead men's bones, and of all uncleanness.
Matthew 23:27

They were zealous for the wrong reasons. Their religious principles were nothing but broken cisterns, and quite evidential of their gross misunderstanding of the truth. They opposed everything that Christ preached, while they remained as spiritually blind as those who had never heard the gospel.

Before his conversion, Paul was a terrorist to the core.

For you have heard of my way of living in time past in the Jews' religion, how that beyond measure I persecuted the assembly of God, and ravaged it. I advanced in the Jews' religion beyond many of my own age among my countrymen, being more exceedingly zealous for the traditions of my fathers.
Galatians 1:13-14, WEB

Paul's zeal for his Jewish beliefs turned him into an enemy of the true worshippers of God, not any different from the twenty-first century bombers and beheaders. And he never saw anything wrong with his actions until the Lord knocked him physically blind, so his spiritual eyes would be opened (Acts 9). If you read the account of his conversion, he said he did what he did, "being zealous for the Lord" (Acts 22:3). He was blinded by zeal.

There's nothing wrong with being zealous for God. But don't use your zeal as a convert-or-croak weapon of intimidation against other faiths. If you do, you have no reward from God. Do you want people to get converted to your religion? Don't kill them. Remember, only living souls can be won to God's kingdom.

e. Spiritual status

In today's world, church leadership is suddenly becoming a profiteering business, with one church leader vying for superiority over the other. Many churches are filled with materialistic ministers, phony pastors, predatory preachers, arrogant apostles, overbearing overseers, dishonest deacons, evil evangelists, and pathetic prophets who give false prophecies.

In their desperate bid for miracles, signs, and wonders, many have gone fetish and are deeply immersed in cultic practices, evoking evil powers to manipulate their members into believing things that are not as if they are. The Bible describes them as, "enemies of the cross of Christ: Whose end is destruction, whose God is their belly, and whose glory is in their shame, who mind earthly things" (Philippians 3:18-19).

Instead of leading souls to heaven, they spoil the souls "through philosophy and vain deceit, after the tradition of men, after the rudiments of the world, and not after Christ" (Colossians 2:8). And who dares correct them? How do you correct someone who has all available versions of the Bible, carries the biggest Bible around, and has read it through more than once? He attended a one-room seminary in America, got a degree from an unknown school of Theology in the United Kingdom, and has those high-sounding prefixes before his name—Apostle, Evangelist, Prophet, Pastor, Doctor, Deacon—all self-conferred.

Some even add JP (Jerusalem Pilgrim) at the end of their names, so people know they've been to Jerusalem and carry a special anointing. They walked the roads that Jesus walked, and prayed under the tree where Jesus prayed. Those are the accolades they use to bamboozle their congregation—poor, innocent souls who're totally ignorant of the danger they're in. Blind members led by blind ministers. "And if the blind lead the blind, both shall fall into the ditch" (Matthew 15:14).

As a believer, "Beware of false prophets, which come to you in sheep's clothing, but inwardly they are ravening wolves" (Matthew 7:15). Beware, so you won't be sorry.

Cure for spiritual blindness

Do you notice any of the above in your life? If so, it's time you sought for a cure. With modern technology, many who're physically blind get a second chance on sight, and can see and function well in life. For spiritual blindness, the only cure is faith

170

in the Lord Jesus. Only He can restore sight to the spiritually blind because He died for the sins of mankind, and the power to recover from spiritual blindness is in His shed blood.

A blind person will need the help of someone with good sight, to help him (her) find his (her) way around. Likewise, it takes knowing Jesus not to miss the way to heaven because He's the Way (John 14:6). He's the sight to the spiritually blind and the everything that a sinner needs to find the way back home. No one follows Him and misses the way. Do you have enough spiritual sight in you to make it to heaven? If not, ask Jesus into your life and you'll never go astray.

5. Christ came to set at liberty them that are bruised

Why would Christ leave His throne of majesty to come and liberate people that are bruised? What's the big deal about bruising? I've been bruised before, many times for that matter. And at no time did I feel that I was in bondage, much less in need of someone to come and liberate me. That was until the Holy Spirit interpreted it to me, and reminded me how bruised I was growing up without a father. Then I understood that Jesus wasn't talking about physical bruises that are visible to the eyes, but emotional bruises that are hidden away deep in the heart.

Sometimes, a sad countenance easily gives a bruised person away. Other times, the emotional distress is completely obscured

171

from easy ocular notice. Many folks look normal on the outside. But inside, they're ticking time bombs, fully loaded with anger and ready to explode at the least provocation. Some, like me, sustained bruises of neglect during their childhood years.

I lived bruised for years because of my father's neglect. For years growing up, my siblings and I never measured up to standard. That created an invisible anger in me toward the man that birthed us and dumped us like worthless rags. I know this may mean little or nothing to some people. After all, why all the fuss about growing up without a father? Well, it was a deal big enough to me.

Do you know that many of the young lives in prisons are there because they lacked parental care, especially fatherly care? Many of them joined gangs because it was the only place they had that sense of acceptance and belonging that every person craves. And before they knew it, their lives spun out of control, with no way forward and no place to go back to. When they later realize how much of life they have wasted, the wound is already deep and it will take the special grace of God to liberate them.

Thank God I had a good mother. But it's bruising for a child watching her mother weep. It's bruising for a child to get sent out of school for unpaid fees. It's bruising for a mother when she doesn't know how the next rent would be paid. It's bruising for a mother when she can't meet the needs of her children. Oh how much we craved just to be happy like the other children around us.

But at one point, we all felt the need to forgive our father, so we could move on with our lives without being tied down to a man who had been dead to us long before he died. It wasn't easy and it didn't happen overnight. But it feels so good to be liberated from those bruises, a liberating experience that only Christ made possible.

To set at liberty them that are bruised. Yes, that was exactly what Christ did for us, one soul at a time. I just told my own story and I'm sure you also have your own story, perhaps similar to mine or completely different.

- You enjoyed the love and care of both parents, but fell into the hands of an abusive spouse.

- A loved one is gone too soon, and the pain is deep, so much so you continue to ask God, why?

- Someone hurt your feelings terribly and you're having a hard time forgiving the person.

- After ruining your life, your lover boy dumped you for another woman.

Mad? Bitter? Miserable? Wounded? Bruised? Yes, you will be all that, and understandably so. But instead of letting it define you or destroy your life, you'll be better off if you release yourself to the Lord, so He can liberate you. There's no need letting your bad past rob you of your good future. Jesus came to liberate us from the pangs of those bruises that may incapacitate us to the point we can no longer enjoy the abundant life that He provided us through His shed blood (John 10:10). Let Him relieve you of your burden and heavy load because that's exactly what He wants to do. He says, "Come to me, all you who labor and are heavily burdened, and I will give you rest" (Matthew 11:28, WEB).

No matter how deep the wound or how bad the bruise, it's no match for the liberating power of the Lord Jesus Christ, for he (she), whom the Son sets free shall be free indeed (John 8:36). Come and join the liberated to sing the song of the liberated. "Free at last, free at last. Thank God Almighty, we are free at last" (Martin Luther King, Jr., 1963).

6. Christ came to preach the acceptable year of the Lord

Hmm!!! So, there's a year that's considered the acceptable year. If that's the case, which year is it? To grasp the full meaning of the "acceptable year," let's go back to the Old Testament, when Prophet Isaiah originally gave this prophecy, and compare it to the New Testament, when Jesus read it in the synagogue.

The Spirit of the Lord God is upon me; because the Lord hath anointed me to preach good tidings unto the meek; he hath sent me to bind up the brokenhearted, to proclaim liberty to the captives, and the opening of the prison to them that are bound; To proclaim the acceptable year of the Lord, and the day of vengeance of our God; to comfort all that mourn.
Isaiah 61:1-2

*When the devil had completed every temptation, he departed from him until another time. Jesus returned in the power of the Spirit into Galilee, and news about him spread through all the surrounding area. He taught in their synagogues, being glorified by all. He came to Nazareth, where he had been brought up. He entered, as was his custom, into the synagogue on the Sabbath day, and stood up to read. The book of the prophet Isaiah was handed to him. He opened the book, and found the place where it was written, "The Spirit of the Lord is on me, because he has anointed me to preach good news to the poor. He has sent me to heal the broken hearted, to proclaim release to the captives, recovering of sight to the blind, to deliver those who are crushed, and to proclaim the acceptable year of the Lord." He closed the book, gave it back to the attendant, and sat down. The eyes of all in the synagogue were fastened on him. He began to tell them, "**Today, this Scripture has been fulfilled in your hearing.**"*
Luke 4:14-21, WEB (Emphasis mine)

At this point, Jesus had overcome Satan's three temptations. On a Sabbath day, very likely the one after the temptations, He went inside the synagogue, sat with the worshippers, did both the scripture reading and the preaching. With all rapt attention on Him, He told the congregants that the prophecy was fulfilled right before their eyes.

In the Old Testament, when liberty was proclaimed in the land, the people celebrated and jubilated because it signified both the restoration of confiscated possessions and the reunion of separated families (Leviticus 25). The year that Christ read that passage in the synagogue was the first year of His earthly ministry. It was the year appointed by God for the work of redemption and salvation of mankind to go into full motion. And Christ was telling those people that they were living witnesses of the day marking the beginning of the mission for which He came to earth, and which was prophesied by Isaiah years before that day.

"Today, this Scripture has been fulfilled in your hearing." As proclaimed liberty marked an end of oppression and separation in the Old Testament, Christ's coming to earth did the same in the New Testament. And for those listening to Him, the day He read that scripture was the day of new beginnings for them. But also new beginnings in your life, in my life, and in the life of every lost soul.

- Once we were blind, but Jesus came and restored our sight.
- Once we were lost, but Jesus came and found us.
- Once we were poor, but Jesus came and made us rich.
- Once we were in bondage, but Jesus came and set us free.
- Once we were brokenhearted, but Jesus came and healed us.
- Once we were bruised, but Jesus came and liberated us.
- Once we were alienated from God, but Jesus came and reconciled us back to God.

*Therefore, even as the Holy Spirit says, "**Today** if you will hear his voice, don't harden your hearts, as in the rebellion, like as in the day of the trial in the wilderness, . . . but exhort one another*

*day by day, so long as it is called "**today**"; lest any one of you be hardened by the deceitfulness of sin. For we have become partakers of Christ, if we hold fast the beginning of our confidence firm to the end: while it is said, "**Today** if you will hear his voice, don't harden your hearts, as in the rebellion."*
Hebrews 3:7-8, 13-15, WEB (Emphases mine)

The day you give your life to Christ and pick up your cross to follow Him marks the beginning of the fulfillment of those purposes for which He came and died for you, and that becomes your, **Today**. Why not make this day your **Today**?

Salvation is liberation from eternal damnation. And, like the return of the prodigal son back home to the father, nothing gladdens the heart of our Savior like the return of a penitent sinner back to the kingdom. It cost Him everything to ensure that no soul is lost. His death on Calvary was the last hurdle He had to cross, and He did that valiantly.

So, with all tasks now completed and with nothing else left to be done for the redemption of mankind, He declared, **"It is finished."** That sure sounds like the first line of a Victory Speech.

Victory Speech

It is finished. Let the world know that on this day and on this hill, every prophecy spoken concerning me and my mission to earth has been fulfilled.

- That I would come into the world, to testify to the truth.
- That Satan would bruise my heel but I would bruise his head.
- That I would be hated without cause and accused by false witnesses.
- That with a kiss from one closest to me, I would be betrayed and sold like a slave for thirty pieces of silver.
- That I would be oppressed and afflicted, smitten and spat upon.
- That I would be led like a lamb to the slaughter and I would not open my mouth.
- That like a sheep before her shearers I would be silent.
- That I would give my back to those who beat me, and my cheeks to those who plucked off the hair.
- That from shame and spitting, I would not hide my face.
- That my enemies would take counsel against me and I would be condemned to death for sins that I never committed.
- That I would be counted with transgressors, and would suffer agony and be stripped naked.
- That my hands and my feet would be pierced, and in my pain, I

would pray for my enemies.

- That my blood would be shed as atonement for the remission of the sins of mankind.

- That in my anguish and sorrow, my friends would stand afar off and my acquaintances would desert me.

- That men would part my garment and cast their lots for it.

- That my strength would be dried up like a potsherd, and my tongue would stick to the roof of my mouth.

- That in my thirst, they would offer me vinegar.

It is finished. I have glorified my Father on earth and I have accomplished all that He sent me to do. I have preached the gospel to the poor and I have healed the brokenhearted. I have preached deliverance to the captives and recovery of sight to the blind. I have set at liberty them that were bruised and I have preached the acceptable year of the Lord to the world.

I have borne the griefs of sinners and I have carried their sorrows. I have been wounded for their transgressions and bruised for their iniquities. By the chastisement placed upon me, I have secured their peace; and by the stripes that I received, I have procured their healing. To those who mourn in Zion, I have given beauty for ashes, the oil of joy for mourning, and the garment of praise for the spirit of heaviness. Henceforth, they shall be called the trees of righteousness.

Foye Adedokun

It is finished. Let the triumph be proclaimed that on this day and on this hill, death was defeated. I have fought the good fight, I have finished my course, I have kept the faith. I have tasted death for everyone and I have given my life as ransom for many. By the shedding of my blood for all people, the blood of bulls and goats will no longer avail for the remission of sins.

Today, the debt for the sins of the entire human race is paid in full.
Today, I lay down my life, that I might take it again.
Today, I render powerless him who had the power of death, that is, the devil.
Today, I have been lifted up from the earth, so I can draw all men unto me.
Today, I have been made higher than the kings of the earth.
Today, the Stone the builders rejected has become the Chief Cornerstone.
Today, death loses its sting and the grave loses its victory.
Today, this perishable body will become imperishable.
Today, this mortal will put on immortality.
Today, the veil of separation between God and man is torn; and henceforth, man will have direct access to My Father through me.

Though I came unto my own and they did not receive me. But those who believe on my name shall receive power to become sons and daughters of my Father. And those who serve me shall be honored by my Father. For their sake I became poor, that through

180

my poverty, they might become rich. I give unto them eternal life and they will never perish. As I am, so they will be in the world and no one will be able to snatch them out of my hand. My Father will be their Father, and my God will be their God. He that hears them hears me; and he that despises them despises me, and my Father that sent me. The works that I did they shall do also. And greater works than I did shall they do.

In my name they shall cast out devils and they shall speak with new tongues. They shall tread on serpents and scorpions, and over all the power of the enemy: and nothing shall by any means hurt them. They shall lay hands on the sick, and they shall recover. They shall be blessed in the city, they shall be blessed in the field. They shall be blessed coming in, they shall be blessed going out. When enemies come against them in one way, they will flee before them in seven ways. And those who rise up against them shall be smitten before their face.

Because they're called by my name, all people of the earth shall be afraid of them. I will make them plenteous in goods and will bless the works of their hands. They shall lend unto many nations, and they shall never borrow. They shall be heads, and not tails. They shall be above only, and never beneath.

I will be with them through the waters, and the rivers shall not overflow them. When they walk through the fire, they shall not be burned, neither shall the flame kindle upon them. I will satisfy their souls in drought, and make fat their bones. They shall be like watered garden, and like a spring of water, whose waters fail not. They shall be unto me a chosen generation, a royal priesthood, a holy nation, a peculiar people; to show forth the praises of him who called them out of darkness into his marvelous light.

In the world they will have tribulations. But they can be of good cheer because I have overcome the world. In blessing I will bless them. In multiplying I will multiply their seeds as the stars of the heaven, and as the sand which is upon the seashore. Their seeds shall possess the gates of their enemies. I will give them power when they're faint, and will increase their strength when they have no might. They will soar high like eagles. When they run, they will not be weary. When they walk, they will not faint.

As I am the vine, they will be the branches. I will leave them with my peace and I will give it unto them, so their hearts will neither be troubled nor fearful. They shall receive power, after that the Holy Ghost is come upon them: and they shall be witnesses unto me both in Jerusalem, and in all Judaea, and in Samaria, and unto the uttermost part of the earth.

I will be their Shephard and Bishop of their souls. They shall be as light to the Gentiles; and would be for salvation to the ends of the earth. And though they shall be hated by all men for my name's sake; those who endure till the end shall be saved.

I am the bread of life. If anyone comes to me, he will not hunger.

I am the light of the world. If anyone follows me, he will not walk in darkness, but will have the light of life.

I am the door. If anyone enters through me, he will be saved.

I am He who has the key of David. When I open, no one can shut. When I shut, no one can open.

I am the Lion of the tribe of Judah, the Root of David, the bright and morning star.

I am the Lamb of God slain to take away the sins of the world.

I am the Sun of righteousness, arising with healing in His wings.

I am the resurrection, and the life, the Alpha and the Omega, the beginning and the end, the first and the last.

I am He who is and who was and who is to come, the Almighty, the Amen, the faithful witness, the firstborn of the dead, and the ruler of the kings of the earth.

It is finished. Now I go to prepare a place for the children of my Father. But I will come back and take them to be with me, that where I am, there they may be also. To them I will grant to sit with me on my throne. They will be arrayed in white garments and will walk with me, for they are worthy. They shall eat of the hidden manna and of the tree of life in the midst of the paradise of my Father. Their names shall be written in the Lamb's book of life and shall not be blotted out.

Foye Adedokun

As I return to Him that sent me, let the testimony be written that I, having loved those who are mine in this world, I have loved them even to the end. My commandment to them is that they love one another, just as I have loved them. And lo, I will be with them even to the end of age.

And now, let the resounding bell of victory ring from coast to coast. The battle is over. The victory is won. And, IT IS FINISHED.

7th Statement:

Father, into thy hands I commend my spirit.

And it was about the sixth hour, and there was a darkness over all the earth until the ninth hour. And the sun was darkened, and the veil of the temple was rent in the midst. And when Jesus had cried with a loud voice, he said, Father, into thy hands I commend my spirit: and having said thus, he gave up the ghost. Now when the centurion saw what was done, he glorified God, saying, Certainly this was a righteous man.

Luke 23:44-47

I wasn't home when my mother departed this earth. But everything I heard pointed to a glorious exit. Few years before she passed, she developed senile dementia and couldn't recollect immediate events. Strangely, she remembered things that happened decades earlier, including her pre-marital years. But as memory-robbed as she was, she never lost memory of her Lord and Savior Jesus Christ.

I was told that three days to the day she died, she made just two statements. "Lord, please take care of my children. Lord, please receive my spirit." She repeated those same words up to minutes before she slept the sleep of the redeemed. Asking the Lord to receive her spirit resonates still, even till this day. How wonderful for a man (woman) to make that his (her) last prayer before death.

Stephen is considered the first Christian martyr. After his

sermon to the good-for-nothing council of elders, he was dragged outside of the city and stoned to death. The Bible records that, as he was being stoned, he prayed, "Lord Jesus, receive my spirit" (Acts 7:9), following in the footsteps of the Savior whose gospel he died for. Our Lord set the precedent for all His followers when He commended His spirit into His Father's hands just before He died. *Father, into thy hands I commend my spirit.*

Compared to how long a person lives, the moment of transition between life and death is very infinitesimal. But when matched against the endlessness of eternity, we know that the grace to pray that short prayer at the end of one's earthly journey is significant for many reasons.

a. It indicates unwavering trust and faith in God

You can't commend your life into the hands of someone you don't trust. Jesus commended His spirit into His Father's hands because He trusted Him. And because of our adoption through salvation, and as heirs of God and joint-heirs with Christ (Romans 8:17), we too can commend our lives into God's hands without fear, just like Christ did on the cross. He says, "Let not your heart be troubled: ye believe in God, believe also in me" (John 14:1).

Committing your life into any other hands is dangerous. Let God have the whole of you—your good times and bad times, your trials and tribulations, in life or in death. Commit everything into His hands and let Him handle it all.

b. It indicates hope of a joyful morning after a sorrowful night

In Psalm 31:5, David prays, "Into thine hand I commit my spirit: thou hast redeemed me, O LORD God of truth." He said that prayer to the same God that Jesus prayed while hanging on the cross. Some people believe it's a bedtime prayer, the kind you pray before laying down to sleep at night, hoping for a good morning the following day. And I love to see it that way, except in a different bedtime sense—asking for a joyful morning in heaven after a sorrowful night on earth.

Christ's life on earth was filled with sorrows. The Bible

says He was "despised and rejected of men; a man of sorrows, and acquainted with grief" (Isaiah 53:3). Not just one sorrow, but sorrows, indicating multiple. But at last, shortly before the journey concluded, He declared, *"Father, into thy hands I commend my spirit."* That declaration followed the three-hour of total darkness over the entire earth.

*And it was about the sixth hour, and **there was a darkness over all the earth until the ninth hour.** And the sun was darkened, and the veil of the temple was rent in the midst. And when Jesus had cried with a loud voice, he said, Father, into thy hands I commend my spirit: and having said thus, he gave up the ghost.*
Luke 23:44-46 (Emphasis mine)

At that moment of commending His spirit into God's hands, His crucifixion turned the day into night. But after giving up the ghost, He transitioned from the night of sorrow into the morning of joy—the joy of overcoming (Revelation 17:14). The Bible says, "Weeping may endure for a night, but joy cometh in the morning" (Psalm 30:5).

Your journey on this planet, no matter how long it lasts, culminates in a night, the final of three stages of life. You were born, you live, you die. And just as you close your eyes at night before sleep, death will close your eyes when the night comes and your life is over. And though the second stage may be filled with weeping because of life's struggles, if you know the Lord, you can rest in peace, knowing that the onset of your night on earth will usher you into a morning of joy in heaven—joy of testimonies and triumphs, joy of freedom from all trials and tribulations, joy of an ever abiding presence with Jesus.

And God shall wipe away all tears from their eyes; and there shall be no more death, neither sorrow, nor crying, neither shall there be any more pain: for the former things are passed away. And he that sat upon the throne said, Behold, I make all things new. And he said unto me, Write: for these words are true and faithful.
Revelation 21:4-5

Nothing on this earth gives lasting joy. But to end up in a place where we will no longer know sorrow is thrilling beyond words. Give Jesus a chance in your life and let Him turn your gloomy night into a glorious morning. And when you sleep the sleep of the redeemed, you're guaranteed the morning of joy after a night of sorrow.

c. It indicates a peaceful ending to a stressful journey

Christ's fourth statement from the cross sounded like a cry of rejection. But His seventh statement was a declaration of a glorious ending to a groaning beginning. From birth and through His entire life, He went from one horrible stress to a more horrible stress, culminating in the most despairing stress of crucifixion. But on Calvary, it all came to a glorious end as He commended His spirit into His Father's hands.

189

Life is an endless cycle of stress, more so for some than others. We barely get through one stress before another one surfaces. But just as every book has a last page, this life will end, and so will the stress we endure. However, the last page of each person's life won't read: The End. It will read: The Beginning. When you reach the end here, where will your beginning be—in heaven or in hell? Will it be one of eternal rest or eternal stress? And if you think this life is stressful, read about hell fire.

And whosoever was not found written in the book of life was cast into the lake of fire.
Revelation 20:15

Think of the Caspian Sea—world's largest lake—as fire, not water. I'm sure you would do anything to avoid getting inside that kind of lake. Now, imagine swimming in it forever, and ever, and ever (Revelation 20:10). At least you know that your labors here on earth will come to a definite end someday. In hell, there's no end. Only those who have been forgiven and redeemed will have eternal rest in heaven. The Bible says, "Blessed are the dead which die in the Lord from henceforth: Yea, saith the Spirit, that they may rest from their labours" (Revelation 14:13).

Make the best decision of your life today. Accept Jesus as your Lord and Savior. And at the end of your earthly journey, you too will be able to say, *Father, into thy hands I commend my spirit.*

d. It indicates Father-child intimacy

Father, into thy hands I commend my spirit. First, He called His Father, then commended His spirit into His hands. That's what happens between father and son who're very close to each other. When you accept Christ as Lord and Savior, you become a legitimate child of God and a bona fide member of God's eternal family.

> *And if children, then heirs; heirs of God, and joint-heirs with Christ; if so be that we suffer with him, that we may be also glorified together.*
> **Romans 8:17**

I love my family, both immediate and extended. And I wish I can have them around me every time. But distance makes that impossible. In heaven, that won't happen because once together, forever together. If you thought Facebook achieved the unthinkable by turning the world into one global village, read this.

Imagine living in a kingdom where God is your Father; and Christ, Peter, James, John, and other saints are your siblings. It'll be awesome beyond words.

> *After this I beheld, and, lo, a great multitude, which no man could number, of all nations, and kindreds, and people, and tongues, stood before the throne, and before the Lamb, clothed with white robes, and palms in their hands.*
> **Revelation 7:9**

In heaven, it will be one family of redeemed souls from all walks of life, with God as the Father of all. There will be no deportation, no hiring or firing, no sorrow, no tears, and no identity theft. It's a stress free kingdom where every soul is kin to every soul, and everybody will understand everybody. But you must be saved to be a part of the glorious family.

e. It indicates absolute surrender to the Higher Power

I'm not a pastor or a theologian. But I've been a child of God long enough to know that surrendering to His will can be tough, especially when things aren't going our way. Just when we try to regain our trust in Him, the devil quickly reminds us how He still hasn't answered our prayer.

At some point on the cross, Christ too felt forsaken by God. But at the end, and contrary to that initial feeling of abandonment, He commended His spirit into God's hands. *Father, into thy hands I commend my spirit.* That was Him saying, *Daddy, whatever is left of me is all yours now. I surrender all to you.*

One great mistake you can make during affliction is to let your temporary problem haze your judgment of the true character of God: that He is and always faithful. Even when life becomes unbearable, remember that some people have been through worse situations, but they maintained their faith and surrendered all to God. You can do the same. Like Job, "Surrender your heart to

God, turn to him in prayer" (Job 11:13). And determine to stay that way. So when your time comes to answer the final call, you too can restfully say, *"Father, into thy hands I commend my spirit."*

f. It means that after the death of the body, the spirit lives on

The idea of being totally dead after death is naturally right, but spiritually wrong.

So also is the resurrection of the dead. . . . It is sown a natural body; it is raised a spiritual body. There is a natural body, and there is a spiritual body.
1 Corinthians 15:42-44

When death occurs and the body becomes lifeless, every body function stops. But whereas the natural body is committed to earth, there's a spiritual body that will be raised back to life to stand before the judgment throne. When that happens, where will your spiritual body go? If you don't have Christ in your life before death, you've already commended your spirit into Satan's hands. When you die, your spiritual body will go to hell fire, where it'll be tortured and tormented forever. But if you're in good standing with the Lord, your spiritual body will go to heaven and dwell in God's presence forever, in bliss and peace.

5

The Criminals

*Repent ye therefore, and be converted, that your sins may be
blotted out, when the times of refreshing shall come from the
presence of the Lord.*
Acts 3:19

Having witnessed so many executions, it was no strange news to the villagers that "three criminals" would be executed on the same day. As Jesus hung on His cross, two real criminals also clung to life on their crosses, one on each side. As their blood dripped and the hours wound down, intense pain and agony eroded all memory of any gratification those two might have enjoyed during their years of criminal activity. Slowly but surely, the reality of death had set in and their lives as they knew it would soon become history.

But something significant, perhaps never heard before in the history of crucifixion, took place on that day on Calvary, when one of the two criminals made a last-ditch attempt at redemption. Chances were he had heard about a man called Jesus from other inmates while incarcerated. After all, how much would it take for such news to travel the entire length and breadth of the village and penetrate all barriers to the ears of the people, including those in prison?

The village probably had its own form of tabloids, the self-appointed and unpaid dispatchers of news. In the absence of printing presses, the noisy markets, fishponds, farmlands, muddy rivers, synagogues, and long and narrow roads, served as readily available platforms to garner as much information as possible from village parrots, and feed them to village gossips. And with feet that moved faster than their old and rusty bikes, news were transmitted at the same speed as the spread of the diseases that ravaged their bodies and the transfer of demons that held their souls in bondage.

The news would be all over the place about the man who claimed to be the Son of God. His mother conceived him while she was still a virgin. He turned people's hearts around, trying to build an army by declaring himself as the only means through which anyone could get to heaven. He claimed to be a king and yet, had no palace. He even said he existed before Abraham (John 8:58), a claim the Jews considered an outrageous and erroneous insult to them.

He also performed all kinds of magic—turning water into wine, walking on water, and raising dead people back to life, one of them from a grave where he'd been buried for four days. Wow!!! The guy must be one-of-a-kind magician.

But I doubt if the criminals knew that the man had been arrested by the Sanhedrin and sentenced to death by crucifixion. And that would mean they had no idea that Christ would be crucified, much less on the same day, at the same time, and in the same place with them. To see the face of the famous man must have been quite amusing for them.

Then in the midst of all the confusion going on around them, one of the thieves heard the man asking God to forgive the monsters that just nailed him to the cross. He immediately sensed there must be more to him than his killers knew, more so considering the crowd and the fanfare that followed him to Calvary. Right there on the cross, his conscience, having been purged by the blood that was being shed for him, could no longer bear his guilt. And almost impromptu, he turned to Jesus and pled: "Lord, remember me when thou comest into thy kingdom" (Luke 23:42).

Was he playing a prank? Was he being sarcastic by calling Him, Lord? No. If he were, he wouldn't rebuke the other thief when he mocked the Lord. Did he just try to see if it would work? No idea. But he knew his life was about to end, and he would go to hell if he didn't make things right with the Man called Jesus. So, in one simple statement, he asked. And in one simple statement, Jesus replied: "Verily I say unto thee, Today shalt thou be with me in paradise" (Luke 23:43).

That moment, the man who had lived a wretched life was

instantaneously hurled out of darkness into God's marvelous light, joining the rank and file of the chosen generation, the royal priesthood, and a whole body of peculiar people (1 Peter 2:9). Yes, it was that simple, easy, and candid.

The greater tendency will be to dismiss those criminals as two individuals who had nothing to offer. But you'll be amazed at the invaluable lessons we can learn from both of their short-lived cross moments—lessons about life, death, and salvation. Please go along with me and let's learn together.

Foye Adedokun

Repentance is the first step to salvation

There are varying claims relative to what comes first before salvation. Some believe that hearing the gospel is the first step to salvation. In that case, why did Judas die a sinner? Judas heard the gospel directly from Jesus' mouth. Yet, he betrayed Him and died a sinner because he never repented of his sins. Other people think that believing in God is the only step to salvation. How then do we explain a religion that uses belief in God to perpetrate evil (John 16:1-2)?

If people believe that killing other people is a service to God, how do we convince them to repent of their actions? That's sternly telling them to quit serving God. I don't think that will be gladly accepted. And we know that no murderer will enter heaven unless he (she) repents of his (her) murderous acts and forsakes them. The Bible explicitly establishes repentance as the sinner's first step to salvation.

Let the wicked forsake his way, and the unrighteous man his thoughts: and let him return unto the Lord, and he will have mercy upon him; and to our God, for he will abundantly pardon.
Isaiah 55:7

Therefore say unto the house of Israel, Thus saith the Lord God; Repent, and turn yourselves from your idols; and turn away your faces from all your abominations.
Ezekiel 14:6

Before Jesus commenced on His ministry, John served as the gospel harbinger. All he preached about was repentance.

In those days came John the Baptist, preaching in the wilderness of Judaea, And saying, Repent ye: for the kingdom of heaven is at hand.
Matthew 3:1-2

And once Jesus began His ministry, His first message was a call to repentance.

From that time Jesus began to preach, and to say, Repent: for the kingdom of heaven is at hand.
Matthew 4:17

During His ministry, He emphasized repentance more than any topic. Here's a dialogue between Him and some unknown individuals. It was on repentance.

*There were present at that season **some** that told him of the Galilaeans, whose blood Pilate had mingled with their sacrifices. And Jesus answering said unto them. . . . except ye repent, ye shall all likewise perish. Or those eighteen, upon whom the tower in Siloam fell, and slew them, think ye that they were sinners above all men that dwelt in Jerusalem? I tell you, Nay: but, except ye repent, ye shall all likewise perish.*
Luke 13:1-5 (Emphasis mine)

To the cities where His works were not appreciated, Jesus spared no effort giving them a bitter bite of the repentance pie.

Then began he to upbraid the cities wherein most of his mighty works were done, because they repented not.
Matthew 11:20

Repentance is forsaking the sinful way of life, to embrace a new and glorious life in Jesus Christ. When the penitent thief made that request to Jesus on the cross, it was out of conviction for his bad life, a conviction that was made more apparent by his sharp rebuke of the unrepentant thief.

But the other answering rebuked him, saying, Dost not thou fear God, seeing thou art in the same condemnation? And we indeed justly; for we receive the due reward of our deeds: but this man hath done nothing amiss.
Luke 23:40-41

Chances were when he was arrested, he just shrugged his shoulder in a casual manner: *Que Será, Será. What will be, will be.* And when he received a death penalty, it didn't come as a surprise. Maybe the other thief was also nonchalant, maybe not. But they both got to Golgotha, where the cross of redemption and reconciliation sandwiched the crosses of rejection unto perdition, and that of repentance unto salvation. And there on the hill, a thief asked the Lord to remember him in His kingdom.

We have no idea if he had ever heard the gospel, or if he believed in God prior to being nailed to the cross. But we sure have an indisputable account of his repentance unto salvation, making him a victorious participant in the only earthly event that receives heaven's applause.

Likewise, I say unto you, there is joy in the presence of the angels of God over one sinner that repenteth.
Luke 15:10

Not joy over hearing the gospel or doing God's service, but joy over repentance. We can only imagine the joy in heaven at that moment when a thief's life became a living testimony of what it truly means for a sinner to repent and be forgiven of his (her) sins.

In one moment

How long do you think it takes for God to transform a person's life or change a situation? I'll say one moment. Think of the saved thief. For him to be sentenced to death by crucifixion, he must have committed a horrible crime, the kind committed by hardened criminals. But in one moment on the cross, he went from a condemned criminal to a redeemed criminal. It was a moment that millions have been reading and preaching about ever since.

The Bible is full of one-moment miracles.

• In one moment, Joseph went from prisoner to prime minister after years of suffering (Genesis 41).

• In one moment, the Israelites' enemies drowned in the Red Sea (Exodus 14).

• In one moment, David conquered Goliath (1 Samuel 17).

• In one moment, the widow of Zarephath's poverty became a thing of the past (1 Kings 17).

• In one moment, abundant provision replaced a long period of terrible famine in Samaria (2 Kings 7).

• In one moment, Legion, a demon-possessed man who lived in the tombs and cut himself with stones, was made whole (Mark 5).

• In one moment, Bartimaeus, a beggar and blind man, received his sight (Mark 10).

• In one moment, the Savior of the world was born (Luke 2).

- In one moment, Peter's night of drought became a morning of draught (Luke 5).

- In one moment, the woman who had been bleeding for twelve years touched the hem of Jesus' garment and was healed (Luke 8).

- In one moment, the woman who had been bent in half for eighteen years was made straight (Luke 13).

- In one moment, a man who had been paralyzed for thirty-eight years was healed (John 5).

- In one moment, a man who was born blind received sight (John 9).

- In one moment, Lazarus walked out of his grave after four days (John 11).

- In one moment, a man who was born lame stood up and walked (Acts 3).

- In one moment, Saul's (Paul) life was changed forever on the road to Damascus (Acts 9).

- And the greatest of all, in one moment, God spoke light into darkness—"Let there be light, and there was light" (Genesis 1).

What darkness is surrounding you right now? How long have you been in that suffering position? Don't give up because God *ain't* through with you yet. Get ready for your one-moment miracle, deliverance, and breakthrough. It doesn't take long for God to turn any situation around. It only takes Him one moment.

Take responsibility for your mistakes

Most people are familiar with that old and lame excuse—the devil made me do it. That was the same excuse our first mother, Eve, gave when God asked why she ate of the tree that He had warned them not to touch.

And the Lord God said unto the woman, What is this that thou hast done? And the woman said, The serpent beguiled me, and I did eat.
Genesis 3:13

I doubt if it took her two seconds to produce that response. Instead of admitting her wrongdoing, she put the blame on Satan. Some blame other people for their personal mistakes. And even worse than that, many blame God, like Adam did in the Garden.

And the Lord God called unto Adam, and said unto him, Where art thou? And he said, I heard thy voice in the garden, and I was afraid, because I was naked; and I hid myself. And he said, Who told thee that thou wast naked? Hast thou eaten of the tree, whereof I commanded thee that thou shouldest not eat? And the man said, The woman whom thou gavest to be with me, she gave me of the tree, and I did eat.
Genesis 13:9-12

Wow!!! He had such a nerve to blame God for giving him a woman as helpmate, instead of admitting his misconduct as a careless head of the Eden household. Aren't we all guilty though? Rather than take responsibility for our actions, if we don't blame others, we blame Satan or God. We don't mind the actions, we just hate the consequences.

Before Ishola Oyenusi was executed in 1971 (see page 105), he confessed that his parents' poverty was what led him to armed robbery because they couldn't afford him a good education. And once he got into robbery, making quick money became so enticing that he could care less about ending innocent lives just to feel rich. But minutes before he was silenced, he said, "I am dying for the offense I have committed" (Nigerian Daily Times, 1971). He took responsibility for his actions.

The story might be similar for the two thieves crucified alongside Jesus. Maybe they didn't even like their lifestyle. Maybe they chose that route to make ends meet due to abject poverty. Maybe they really wanted to be good citizens, but didn't know what to do. Maybe if someone had come to their rescue, their story would have been different. Maybe, maybe, just maybe. Anything could have pushed them into stealing.

Please don't misunderstand me. I'm not and will never be in support of the kind of life they lived. But I know for certain that life can push people to do what they won't do under normal circumstances. And that's the more reason why I admire the saved thief's courage to take the blame for his actions.

In a simple, yet straightforward way, he accepted his fate and wasted no time setting the other guy straight. *"For we receive the due reward of our deeds.*" He knew he was responsible for the predicament he was in. He probably wished he could undo his mistakes, that he could go back and start all over again. Regretfully, it was too late. And though bad to be in that painful position, but better not to blame somebody else, for that would be another gaffe.

After committing adultery with Bathsheba and getting her pregnant, David came up with a more cruel plan to cover up his sin. He killed Uriah, Bathsheba's husband. That was a double whammy offense. But when he came to his senses, he didn't blame anyone but himself. He went before God and begged for mercy.

Have mercy on me, God, according to your loving kindness. According to the multitude of your tender mercies, blot out my transgressions. Wash me thoroughly from my iniquity. Cleanse me from my sin. For I know my transgressions. My sin is constantly before me. Against you, and you only, have I sinned, and done that which is evil in your sight; that you may be proved right when you speak, and justified when you judge.
Psalm 51:1-4, WEB

Regardless of age or status, no one is above mistake. But let's take a que from the saved thief's life and not pass the blame on someone else. The Bible says, "He who conceals his sins doesn't prosper, but whoever confesses and renounces them finds mercy." (Proverbs 28:13, WEB). Don't blame anyone for your mistakes. When you're wrong, you're wrong. *Caso cerrado.* Case closed.

Salvation has no platform

Starting a ministry these days is sadly becoming more of a commercial vocation than it is spiritual conviction. You don't need any divine calling or special leading to start a church. Just have a fake charm, a rehearsed winsome smile, some nice twisting and turning, a flurry of high-sounding words, and a good appearance, even if you have to borrow a suit from a stranger. And in no time, you will be preaching a message of doom to the deluded members of your doomed ministry.

Years ago in Nigeria, there were only few churches, with great peace and stability. Today, turn to any corner and there's at least one church, if not more, with some of those churches boasting of thousands of worshippers in one service. In fact, there are shopping complexes, where almost every store has been converted to a church, defeating the purpose for which the complex was built.

But the evil being perpetrated in the country on daily basis makes even the dullest mind want to question the efficacy of the presence of those places of worship, places of prayer, places where God's name is exalted above all other names. That's not surprising because the weightier matters of the kingdom have been neglected, and the focus has shifted from spiritual growth to denominational superiority.

Every denomination has its own spiritual bylaws, with so many beliefs, principles, dos, and don'ts, which are as complicated as they are befuddling. Those generally self-conceited bylaws are imposed upon the congregation and presented as the ultimate best for eternal security; and any deviation from them is a bon voyage to hell. To the brainwashed members of a certain denomination, any claim of salvation outside of their church is not recognized by God. Even if you're born again, you must come to their church and be **reborn** again, if you wish to make heaven.

In one denomination, wedding gowns, rings, and cakes are okay. In another denomination, they're contrabands from hell. In one denomination, no lotion or nice powder allowed, because, to the spirit-filled worshippers, they smell like fragrance from the dungeon of demons. In another denomination, the pastor asks his members to take few minutes every service to admire each other's looks, no matter how outlandish or seductive.

The instruments that some preachers condemned as satanic several years ago have become key channels of evangelism in their ministry, and members now have them conspicuously displayed in their houses. Those instruments are suddenly not satanic anymore. That's spiritual flip-flopping, which is not found in Christ. The Bible says, "Jesus Christ the same yesterday, and to day, and for ever" (Hebrews 13:8). He is today, what He was yesterday, and will be tomorrow—the Savior of the world.

The purpose of salvation is defeated when it's solely based on church membership and stringent allegiance to denominational doctrines. There are underground preachers who have no pillows to lay their heads on, preachers who're always in harm's way and within arm's reach of danger, preachers who have no pulpits or church buildings, preachers who've lost all things for the sake of winning others to Christ, preachers who care more about Christ's ministry than they do about church membership. Yet, thousands get saved through them because they risk everything for kingdom sake. And unquestionably, they and their converts will make heaven as yours truly as the thief saved on the cross.

That guy had no church membership, belonged to no denomination, had no priest standing beside him to administer the last holy communion. All he had was a temporary cross on which he hung, and my dear Lord with whom he'll spend eternity. But he possessed the only platform for salvation—a changed heart. That's all that is required to be with Christ in His kingdom. You can belong to any church or denomination you want. If your heart isn't right with God, you're going to hell.

Please I'm not promoting an incentive to avoid being part of a church. As a Christian, I'll question your salvation if you don't belong to a Bible-believing church, where true gospel message is placed above any other thing. Just as the eye can't shun the other parts of the body, you can't claim to be a member of the body of Christ and disregard associating with other believers (Hebrews 10:25). On the other hand, the salvation of a soul can't be confined to within the four walls of brick-and-mortar. A soul can be saved anywhere, in any place, under any circumstance, and through any other saved soul—pastor or no pastor, preacher or no preacher, priest or no priest.

As many souls can be saved in a prison as in a palace, as many in a dungeon as in a desert, as many inside a plane as on a ship. God can use a judge to save a soul inside a court, the same way He uses a pastor inside the church. Why? Because salvation has nothing to do with the platform, but has everything to do with the person. Hey, if a soul can be saved on a cross, a soul can be saved anywhere.

Singled out for a reason

I've heard and read about situations where the only rational explanation for what happened was divine or supernatural intervention. Such situations like the mysterious rescue of a baby from a ghastly auto accident that left every adult passenger dead; a totaled vehicle where the driver escaped without a scratch; a woman without a womb who gave birth to two healthy babies; or a sickle cell patient, who had suffered tremendous pain her entire life, only to be told at her next doctor's visit that her blood had been cleared of the disease, leaving the doctor in limbo of even the remotest possible medical explanation. And from that moment, she was totally healed and has been living pain-free.

In the Bible, we read about individuals who were singled out for divine purposes.

Abraham was singled out for divine procreation.

Joseph was singled out for divine promotion.

Moses was singled out for divine leadership.

David was singled out for divine victory.

Elijah was singled out for a divine translation to heaven.

Daniel was singled out for divine interpretation of dreams.

Esther was singled out for divine favor.

Solomon was singled out for divine wisdom.

Noah was singled out for divine preservation of human race.

Rahab was singled out for divine protection of God's men.

Foye Adedokun

Mary was singled out for divine conception of the Savior.

John was singled out for divine assignment to take care of Mary.

Peter was singled out for divine commission.

Paul was singled out for a divine calling.

But it wasn't only human beings. In this passage, a fish was singled out for divine provision.

And when he was come into the house, Jesus prevented him, saying, What thinkest thou, Simon? of whom do the kings of the earth take custom or tribute? of their own children, or of strangers? Peter saith unto him, Of strangers. Jesus saith unto him, Then are the children free. Notwithstanding, lest we should offend them, go thou to the sea, and cast an hook, and take up the fish that first cometh up; and when thou hast opened his mouth, thou shalt find a piece of money: that take, and give unto them for me and thee.
Matthew 17:25-27

When Jesus asked Peter to go to the sea, He instructed him to open the mouth of the first fish. But have you ever considered the scanty details of that errand? On two previous occasions when Peter caught a draught of fishes following the Lord's command (Luke 5:1-6; John 21:1-7), Jesus was present at the shore and He was specific about where to cast the hook. But with the coin-fish catch, He was neither there with Peter, nor specific about the exact spot to toss the hook. Peter—and most likely all by himself—was to go and cast his hook to the sea. That was it. No other details. Asking him to go and look for a coin by the shore seemed like an easier errand. And from human perspective, anything could have gone wrong.

If I were to give a rough estimate of the number of fishes in that sea, I'll say one fish for every villager. That would still be thousands of fishes. Nobody knows how far that fish traveled to get to that spot, no idea how long the coin was in the fish's mouth, and no idea how many fishes raced to Peter's hook. But this much we know.

That particular fish picked the coin and held it in its mouth until Peter caught it. It was the first fish Peter pulled up. And when he opened its mouth, he found the coin and he removed it, just as the Lord asked him to do. Considering the vastness of the sea and the many fishes therein, there's only one explanation we can give for the miracle—Divine orchestration. That catch was no fluke. The calculated accuracy was supernatural, far from a stroke of luck. Of all the fishes in the sea, that fish was singled out to provide the coin that Jesus would use to settle the temple tax.

The two thieves on the crosses were two of many criminals in the village. But why those two on Golgotha, same day and same time with Jesus? Why did one thief repent and the other did not? If more criminals were crucified at that same time and place, could we have had more on-the-cross-salvation miracles to read about? All good imaginative questions arising from personal interest.

But because of my strong belief in destiny, I think that

moment was meant for that thief, and it was no accident or sheer coincidence that he was crucified alongside Jesus. Fate pulled him out of the abyss of moral decadence and placed him beside Jesus, where his eternal destiny was changed, forever. He was singled out for divine salvation. *Sin estrés ni sudor.* No stress, no sweat.

I'm not implying that God purposely chose the saved thief over the unsaved one. To think that way would be tantamount to claiming that God is partial. However, I absolutely believe that the way He chooses to perform His wonders in the life of His creatures is totally up to Him, and no man is qualified to challenge Him. His thoughts are not our thoughts, and His ways are not our ways (Isaiah 55:8). The Bible says, "He does according to his will in the army of heaven, and among the inhabitants of the earth; and none can stay his hand, or ask him, What are you doing?" (Daniel 4:35, WEB).

Jesus says of the widow of Zarephath, "But truly I tell you, there were many widows in Israel in the days of Elijah, when the sky was shut up three years and six months, when a great famine came over all the land. Elijah was sent to none of them, except to Zarephath, in the land of Sidon, to a woman who was a widow" (Luke 4:25-26). Why that widow out of the widows in Israel? Divine purpose. Why a poor widow who was counting on the little she had as her last meal? Divine purpose. Of all the possible better choices, God overlooked her poverty and picked her to provide sustenance for His servant, Elijah. And because she obeyed, the divine provision bounced back to her. She never lacked food again.

How about Peter? Jesus says to him, "And I say also unto thee, That thou art Peter, and upon this rock I will build my church; and the gates of hell shall not prevail against it. And I will give unto thee the keys of the kingdom of heaven: and whatsoever thou shalt bind on earth shall be bound in heaven: and whatsoever thou shalt loose on earth shall be loosed in heaven" (Matthew 16:18-19).

That was the same Peter who, because of incontinent rage, used a sword to chop off Malchus' right ear (John 18:10). It was the same Peter who denied Jesus three times within the span of two cockcrows (Luke 22). It was the same Peter who hardly waited for Christ to resurrect before going back to his old fishing job (John 21). Why would Jesus build His glorious church on such a lousy rock? Well, I think a

Even in the most illogical situation, God can single you out for a divine purpose.

more pertinent question should be, why would Christ die for someone like me? If my own sins had been counted against me, I would have been doomed forever.

Regardless of where you are in life, there's no reason to think that God can no longer single you out for His glory. Like the fish was singled out for divine provision, like Joseph was singled out for divine promotion, like the thief on the cross was singled out for divine salvation, like Peter was singled out for a divine commission, ask God to single you out for a divine purpose.

If He singles you out for divine leadership, you'll be an unquestionable authority in any position He puts you. If He singles you out for divine promotion, the exponential rate at which you're being promoted will leave others speechless. If He singles you out for divine wisdom, kings and nobles will want to hear your opinion. If He singles you out for divine preaching, all you need do is open your mouth and He will fill it with His message. If He singles you out for divine prosperity, anything you lay your hands upon to do will prosper. If He singles you out for divine anointing, there will be signs and wonders anywhere you go.

May the Lord single you out for a divine purpose. May He give you a divine connection with the right people who will help to fulfill His purpose in your life. And, at the right time, may He put you in that place where your destiny will be changed for the best, in Jesus' Name.

When the enemy's plan works for your good

Because it's very unnatural for an enemy to be good, no one should expect anything good from an enemy. Guess what? You have every right to feel that way, if you do. But please let me remind you that our God is a Master strategist. And He can use your enemy—seen and unseen, known and unknown—to get you to your victory and the location of your destiny. Time and again, the plan of the enemy in an individual's life has been turned around for the good of the individual.

We know the story of Joseph—how his brothers conspired and sold him to the Midianites merchantmen (Genesis 37). They had no idea God was using them to transport Joseph to that place where his dreams of greatness would come to pass. Though Joseph suffered years of oppression from those he knew not, God turned everything around when he, against all odds, became a prime minister in a strange land of Egypt.

When his enemy-brothers saw him years later, they were so overtaken by fear that they "fell down before his face; and they said, Behold, we be thy servants" (Genesis 50:18). If they knew how wonderful the end would be for Joseph, they would not have sold him into slavery.

Sometimes, God moves your enemies to rise up against you, so He can deal with them once and for all. Do you think it was a coincidence that Pharaoh, after releasing the Israelites, rose up and chased after them? No, it wasn't. That was God's strategy to bring a permanent end to the enemies that had tormented His chosen people for over four centuries (Exodus 14). Were the Israelites scared? Yes, they were.

And when Pharaoh drew nigh, the children of Israel lifted up their eyes, and, behold, the Egyptians marched after them; and they were sore afraid: and the children of Israel cried out unto the LORD.
Exodus 14:10

But read what their leader, Moses, said to them.

And Moses said unto the people, Fear ye not, stand still, and see the salvation of the LORD, which he will shew to you to day: for the Egyptians whom ye have seen to day, ye shall see them again no more for ever.
Exodus 14:13

Following that was the parting of the Red Sea, the two-way miracle that saved the Israelites and drowned their enemies. Had Pharaoh and his army not pursued the Israelites, they would not have drowned in the Red Sea. And the Israelites might still be haunted by the fear of the enemies they left behind.

There's one principal enemy, Satan. He's the enemy of the entire human race and his one desire is to send every soul to hell, exploiting whatever strategy it'll take to realize his goal. Satan wanted to destroy the thief's life by exploiting either his greed or poverty to afflict him with stealing. And that he was sentenced to death by crucifixion proves that his crimes were awful. But what Satan meant for evil turned out for God's glory. When that guy was nailed to the cross, Satan probably thought he had won. Little did he know that his plan to destroy the criminal's soul would, at the final countdown of his life, put him side by side with the Savior; neither did he think that a man, who, up until his execution, lived a conscience-void life, would suddenly be overtaken by conscience and be humble enough to turn to Christ for help.

If naked eyes could behold Satan and his cohorts, I bet one moment, they were high-fiving to celebrate their victory over the thief's soul. And the next moment, they were lamenting their woe as the criminal turned to Jesus and asked to be with Him in His kingdom; and even more disappointed that Jesus would grant the request of such a vagabond. With his own evil tactics, Satan pushed the thief to his cross of salvation.

The enemy didn't create you and he wasn't there when God formed you. Don't be so engrossed thinking about what the bad enemy has done to you, that you miss out on what the good Lord wants to do for you. The plan of the enemy to demote you, God will use it to promote you. The plan of the enemy to end your life, God will use it to save your life. Whatever the enemy lays up against you, God will turn it around for your good. God, not the enemy, has the final say over your life.

Faith based on expectations is a danger to salvation

That's a mouthful truth. The reason many souls will miss heaven is because they base their faith on the assumption of what should be or not be. Going back to the unsaved thief, the reason he missed paradise was because he had a wrong assumption about Jesus.

> *And one of the malefactors which were hanged railed on him,*
> *saying, If thou be Christ, save thyself and us.*
> **Luke 23:39**

That was his way of saying, *Show me what you can do, and I'll believe who you claim to be.* That statement underscored his carnality, insensitivity, skepticism, haughty spirit, hardened heart, unbridled tongue, and lack of reverence for God. He lost eternity in paradise because his faith was based on expectations. He used the crucifixion to judge the crucified. He misunderstood Christ's humility in not saving Himself as His inability to save Himself. Because he lacked all knowledge about the Man in the middle, He wanted to see a miracle to believe the miracle worker.

If Christ had done something magical on the cross, like commanding fire on His assailants or making it impossible for the nails to penetrate His hands and feet, maybe he too would have repented. But for him, if Christ "could not" save Himself, He certainly could not save him. He missed a golden opportunity to be saved and he died a sinner. He thought it was cool to mock the Savior. He would get to hell before realizing that his cool joke had no place in the hot fire.

The saved thief knew better. He didn't define Jesus' power by the pierced hands and feet, the dripping blood, the moans and groans of pain and anguish coming from a Man who possessed enough power to bring the dead back to life. He bypassed a wrong assumption of what Christ should have done to prove Himself, and

God may not prove His power the way we expect, or, at the time we expect. But that doesn't make Him any less God than He was, is, and forever will be.

instead, held on to the strong assurance of what He could do, even in that posture that some misinterpreted as an evidence of His "powerlessness."

The Bible says if we ask, we shall receive (Matthew 7:7-8; 21:22). And for the most part, our faith rests on that assumption. But how do we explain when we ask and don't receive, seek and don't find, knock and the door is locked, bolts and latches? It's a troubling question, especially for people who have been trusting God for years.

Based on my own muddled assumption of perfect timing, there's no reason why God can't do it right away, because, for me, the most perfect time is *right now*. All God needs do is blow His breath and the answers to my prayers will be flowing in like a river. On occasions when that didn't happen, I was disappointed. But in hindsight, what I called a delay turned out to be the perfect timing,

Foye Adedokun

and even more glorifying than what I prayed for. Now I know that the time I need to trust God the most is when I'm having a hard time trusting Him.

Our expectations can be disappointed, and things may not work out the way we want. But it doesn't mean that God is no longer God or can no longer be trusted. If our faith is based only on guaranteed answers to prayers, it'll be difficult to rebound when that doesn't happen. No matter how gloomy the situation looks, don't let your circumstances turn you into a pessimist. Never base your faith in God on your expectations of what He should do or not do. Love and trust Him because of Who He is, and not because of what you want.

Salvation day for one, damnation day for the other

No number of gospel messages preached, no number of crusades conducted, no number of churches built, and indeed, no number of warnings given, those who are determined not to change won't change.

Consider the two thieves. One thief asked for paradise, the other thief asked for a proof. One was sorry, the other was scornful. One repented, the other ridiculed. Was there something the saved thief saw or heard that the unsaved thief missed? I don't think so. They both witnessed the events and they both heard Jesus pray for His killers. The saved thief even preached a quick sermon to the unsaved one.

And one of the malefactors which were hanged railed on him, saying, If thou be Christ, save thyself and us. But the other answering rebuked him, saying, Dost not thou fear God, seeing thou art in the same condemnation? And we indeed justly; for we receive the due reward of our deeds: but this man hath done nothing amiss.
Luke 23:39-41

That sharp rebuke should have made him rethink his stance. Sadly, it entered through one ear and egressed through the other. Two individuals, same lifestyle, same distance from the Savior, same death, but different eternal fates. Though so close to each other in life, in eternity they will be as far from each other as heaven is from hell. What went down in history as the day of salvation for one, went down as the day of damnation for the other.

There were probably hundreds, if not thousands, of people on Calvary, who came to have the last laugh at the criminals that had pestered their lives for years. And there would be those who went there out of disbelief, to confirm the rumor that the Man who performed all those miracles would in fact die by crucifixion. It's not even unlikely that some people anticipated the moment when Jesus would turn into a white bird and fly away. Whatever the reasons that brought them there, there was one thing that each person on that hill shared with the three men on the crosses—death.

You live in a gold-adorned palace, waited on and served at will by men like you. Though they're believers, their low status makes you naturally deaf to the message of salvation they try so hard to share with you. After all, what can people like them tell someone like you? They're just your servants.

Well, let me remind you that one day, death, the master leveler, will relieve you of your status and put you in a six-foot hole, just as the person who served you your entire life. Whether we admit it or dismiss the thought of it, we'll die. I will die, you will die, all of us will die.

To every thing there is a season, and a time to every purpose under the heaven: A time to be born, and a time to die.
Ecclesiastes 3:1-2

Death is an inevitable end for all. I'm sure there are people who possess enough wealth to bribe death, so they can live for as long as they want. But nothing that you have can stop death when it's time because it's beyond human control.

There is no man that hath power over the spirit to retain the spirit;
neither hath he power in the day of death.
Ecclesiastes 8:8

I resent the lifestyle that those two thieves chose, same way I resent the life Paul lived pre-conversion. And I feel sorry for any of their victims who died unsaved. At one point, they too died. But for the unsaved thief, it was his doomsday; and for Paul and the saved thief, the birth of a glorious dawn in paradise.

Like them, every person has only one of two options. I've made my choice, to stick it out till I see my Savior on the throne. But to think that a day is coming when I'll see both Paul and the penitent thief in heaven puts me over the moon, and makes it a reunion greatly anticipated. When I depart from here, both of them will be waiting to welcome me home.

When your time on earth is done and your day of reckoning is here, what fate awaits you on the other side? Will it be a day of deliverance or a day of doom? Will it be glory in heaven or gloom in hell? Will it be a day of eternal salvation or a day of eternal damnation? *Selah.*

Foye Adedokun

Seek ye the LORD while he may be found, call ye upon him while he is near.
Isaiah 55:6

But seek ye first the kingdom of God, and his righteousness; and all these things shall be added unto you.
Matthew 6:33

It is appointed unto men once to die, and after this the judgment.
Hebrews 9:27

Make the decision for your salvation now. Don't wait another minute because the next minute you wait may be your last minute on earth. Delay is dangerous.

Nature of death has no bearing on eternity with Jesus

I questioned God on numerous instances when I heard or read about believers, who served Him wholeheartedly, only to die in tragic ways like plane crash, road accidents, fire, homicide. I struggled with that notion because I believed that profession of faith in Christ should give automatic protection from any form of tragic death.

Then I remembered the disciples of the Lord, who died horrific deaths. I remembered John the Baptist, Christ's forerunner, who was beheaded by Herod. I remembered Stephen, advocate of the gospel, who was stoned to death. I remembered fellow brethren, whose illnesses and diseases defied all intercession for healing till they crossed over to glory. I remembered pastors and ministers of God, who prayed for the sick and they recovered. But when they took ill, the prayers of their entire congregation could not save them from dying. I remembered my Savior, the Son of God, and indeed, God Himself, who died the most brutal and excruciating death on a cross of shame and injustice. Then I realize that the type of death a saint dies means nothing to God.

The Bible says, "Precious in the sight of the Lord is the death of his saints" (Psalm 116:15). The death is precious. But how we die is irrelevant. The world is an evil place and a battlefield. That's why the death of a saint (saved soul) is precious in God's sight because it marks a safe return from a danger zone.

227

Foye Adedokun

Let's try this analogy.

Two siblings, brother and sister, are out on a short trip. On reaching their destination, their enthusiasm turns sour as trouble breaks out and they get separated trying to escape. Eventually, they both get home to the father and try to narrate their ordeal.

Do you think their father will care about what the trouble is or how they each make it home? No. And it's not because he doesn't care about them while away from him. But once they're home, their safe return is the only important part of their trip, rendering the hurdles of the journey of no relevance to the happy reunion. The filial bond he shares with them makes them precious to him and he's beyond glad to have them safely back in his bosom of love. Precious in his sight is the return of his dear children.

If you're saved, you're God's child and a saint. And the death of any saint—like the saved thief, like Abraham, like Elijah and Elisha, like Paul, like Peter, like Stephen, like Pastor Sam, and like my mother—is a safe return back home to Him, and it's precious in His sight. How we escape from this life of turmoil is irrelevant. Making it home to heaven saved and redeemed is the joy of the journey, because, after all said and done, it's the only thing that will matter at the end of our lives here on earth.

At the end of your life's journey, may your death be precious in God's sight, in Jesus' Name.

Pre-death decision determines post-death destination

Doctrine of election is an asinine belief that some people are destined for heaven and others are destined for hell, a pre-birth pronouncement that nothing can change. That's heresy and it's far from the truth found in God's word.

*For God so loved the world, that he gave his only begotten Son, that **whosoever** believeth in him should not perish, but have everlasting life.*
John 3:16 (Emphasis mine)

Why would God send His only Son to come and die for a sinner if the sinner's fate is already sealed before birth? And why would Christ agree to come and die for sinners, if His death is of no use to the remission of sins? Pure garbage. Even if Satan has sealed a person's fate for hell, God provided a way for such evil fate to be reversed through the shed blood of Jesus Christ. And the choice of getting saved or not is a personal decision.

Bottom line is, the reason some people will make heaven is the same reason others will miss it—faith or no faith in the Lord Jesus Christ. To the saved thief, Jesus had the power to take him to paradise. To the unsaved thief, Jesus lacked the power to take him to paradise. The repentant thief made it because he had faith in the saving power of the Lord Jesus. The unrepentant thief missed it because he lacked faith in the saving power of the Lord Jesus.

For the preaching of the cross is to them that perish foolishness; but unto us which are saved it is the power of God. For the Jews require a sign, and the Greeks seek after wisdom: But we preach Christ crucified, unto the Jews a stumblingblock, and unto the Greeks foolishness; But unto them which are called, both Jews and Greeks, Christ the power of God, and the wisdom of God.
1 Corinthians 1:18, 22-24

To some folks, your decision to accept Christ is foolish. The gospel that you heard and believed, they heard it and never believed. You think you're wise surrendering your life to Christ, they think you're foolish believing such old fables. And God forbid you move up to the next level—preaching and winning souls—then they think you're a special kind of fool. But the Bible says, "The fool hath said in his heart, There is no God" (Psalm 14:1). And "He that winneth souls is wise" (Proverbs 11:30). It means the person who doesn't believe in God and doesn't win souls is the fool.

As millions are going to heaven because they receive Christ, millions are going to hell because they reject Him. Regrettably, they will get there before realizing the great wisdom in what they call foolishness. Don't let death be the beginning of your eternal regret. Ignore all foolish noises and focus on your salvation. The saved thief made that decision before he died because he knew it would be too late after death. Do what is right now, so you too can be with Jesus in His kingdom.

God can bring the best out of the worst situation

Golgotha. One day in its history, that hill welcomed people plagued by a myriad of problems: Physical affliction, demonic oppression, disappointment, sorrow, emotional affliction, suffering, broken hearts, anguish, diseases, hopelessness, and indeed, every form of the other end of a good and happy life. One of them was a thief, whose life, as the crowd thought, had come to a terrible end. But somehow, somehow, he pulled through a dark tunnel to an eternal light.

Maybe he lived a bad life till the day he was apprehended. Or, maybe it was just one heinous crime that led to his abysmal fate. We'll never know. But it's incredible that such a terrible life could have such a terrific end. It was a distinctive case of God bringing the best out of the worst.

We already know that Mary followed Jesus to Calvary. Though it's hard to imagine how she felt seeing her Son on the cross, but at least she knew He wasn't a criminal, a claim that the thief's parents could not make. We don't know if his parents were dead or alive, if they were on Golgotha, or deliberately absent from the hill because of shame. But let's just assume they were still living.

No matter how bad the thief was, he was still their son. Imagine their pain, knowing that their son was hanging on the cross for a crime. They knew it was over for him. All hope was lost.

There was nothing anyone could do to salvage whatever was left of their savage criminal son. He lived bad and he would die bad, or so they thought because, in the twinkling of an eye, the man whose life had been written off as hopeless, received the greatest hope in life—eternity with Jesus.

The story is the same for any sinner because God's love, mercy, and forgiveness is without reservation. Otherwise, folks like the following should never be mentioned as people of faith.

Jacob—evil plotter and stealer of blessings (Genesis 25-36).

Moses—documented murderer (Exodus 2).

Rahab—a harlot (Joshua 2-6).

Samson—adulterer and lover of strange women (Judges 14, 16).

David—adulterer cum murderer (2 Samuel 11).

Yet, the Bible lists them alongside spiritual Hall of Famers like Abraham, Sarah, Noah, Enoch, and Gideon (Hebrews 11). But it wasn't because of the way any of them started, but because of the way each of them finished.

Therefore if any man be in Christ, he is a new creature: old things are passed away; behold, all things are become new.
2 Corinthians 5:17

Some children lack the teachable spirit. They're determined to travel the route of their own choosing, not minding what could be the dire consequence of their actions. Maybe that was the case with the thief on the cross, leaving his parents perplexed and devastated after several attempts to rehabilitate him. And as expected, they got tired and gave up.

Perhaps as a parent, you're in a similar situation. You've tried everything parentally possible to make your child live right, but to no avail. The problem is already beyond your power and you have written him (her) off as a worst-case scenario. As a fellow parent, I know that's a hard place to be. But do you know that only death brings an end to any hope in life?

For there is hope of a tree, if it be cut down, that it will sprout again, and that the tender branch thereof will not cease. Though the root thereof wax old in the earth, and the stock thereof die in the ground; Yet through the scent of water it will bud, and bring forth boughs like a plant.
Job 14:7-9

I've heard testimonies of children who got converted long after the death of their parents. Some said their mothers never gave up praying for their salvation. Others describe the agony of their fathers' struggles to give them good life, which never happened in their lifetime. But in the end, those prayers and struggles were not in vain because their wishes were granted, though posthumously.

It's hard to believe that a criminal's life would be changed on the cross of all places. In fact, majority of the crowd might not be aware of what was going on between him and Jesus. Those who noticed could have dismissed it as mere last-minute *tête-à-tête* between two criminals who were both very close to their deaths.

233

And if anyone heard the conversation, they probably had no clue what it meant. But Jesus understood and the thief understood. Halleluyah!!!

As long as the person you're praying for is alive, don't stop believing because there's hope for redemption. God will not put you to shame. Maybe it's your child. Satan doesn't want him (her) to succeed or to be saved. Each time you intercede and pray for him (her), all hell breaks loose and a battle line is drawn. Don't give up. Persist in prayer without ever relenting or doubting. Just know that God will bring the best out of that child that you see as the worst thing that ever happened to you. He did it for Paul. He did it for the armed robber turned Evangelist in my country, who, by the grace of God, I had the honor to entertain in my house, something I wouldn't dare prior to his salvation.

Praying for someone's salvation is a warfare. And the odds of getting discouraged are high when it's taking too long. But to give up is to concede victory to Satan.

On Calvary, God brought the best out of a most worthless life, when a condemned thief became a saved thief that generations of pastors and preachers have been preaching about ever since. The same God can, and will, do it for you.

And that applies to any area of your life that you consider dead and hopeless. God can turn it around for the best. Jacob never knew he would see his "dead" son, Joseph, again. From the time

Joseph's brothers went home and told their father that Joseph had been killed by a wild beast, it took almost twenty years before he set his eyes on him again. He didn't even know Joseph was still alive. After all, a wild beast had devoured him, leaving only his cherished coat of many colors as the reminder of his terrible death. But out of that supposedly tragic, heartbreaking, sad, hopeless, and dead situation emerged a living prime minister in a foreign land, whom God later used to feed the entire family during a severe famine.

That child that is struggling academically may become a famous billionaire in life. That unbelieving and abusive spouse may become a preacher and the best spouse later in life. That business that is dragging today may become an empire tomorrow. That breakup with your boyfriend (girlfriend) may be God's way of preserving you for the right person He has coming your way. That physical challenge that seems to be holding you down may be the very thing that God will use to catapult you into fame. The great Redeemer and Restorer of souls can bring the best out of the worst situation.

Man's court versus God's court

Over thirty years ago in Nigeria, our house fellowship group leader led a man to Christ during one of his prison ministration visits. The man had spent years on death row for murder. But after his salvation, he changed completely and lived true to Paul's words: "Therefore if any man be in Christ, he is a new creature: old things are passed away; behold, all things are become new" (2 Corinthians 5:17).

When told of his execution date, he sent a letter to our fellowship leader, to thank him for leading him to Christ, and helping him to secure a better life that he was looking forward to at the end of his life here on earth. Our leader brought the letter to fellowship and asked members to pray for God's prompt and divine intervention. And he determined to do anything he could to have the sentence reversed, considering the years that man had spent behind bars. God heard our prayer and his death sentence was commuted to life. And if I remember correctly, he was released few years into his life sentence because of his excellent character.

A similar scenario took place here in America, about an individual on death row. Testimonies about that person's changed life prompted thousands of people and prominent dignitaries to petition the governor of that state to spare the individual's life. But the governor declined and the execution went as scheduled.

Two identical cases in two continents that are eon miles from each other. One was reversed, the other was retained.

According to Romans 6:23, all spiritual sinners receive the same verdict—death. The verdict is irrespective of who you are. But, unlike the sentence from man, which may or may not be reversed, the sentence from God will be reversed and commuted to life in heaven if the sinner repents. What happens in the court of man is different from what happens in God's court.

In man's court	In God's court
Your guilty verdict may be a mistake.	There's no mistake about your guilty verdict.
You're presumed innocent until proven guilty.	You will remain guilty until forgiven.
You can only appear before the Judge on a given date, time, and place.	You can appear before Him any day, anytime, anywhere.
You employ the services of an attorney to represent you and plead your case before the Judge.	You go directly before Him to beg for forgiveness and the Holy Spirit will be your advocate.
You pay your attorney for services rendered.	No payment required because Jesus already paid it all in advance of your sins.
Your plea for pardon is subject to the Judge's approval, which may or may not be favorable, depending on the Judge's discretion, knowledge, and sometimes, mood.	God Himself is the Judge and His forgiveness is guaranteed upon your repentance.
You beg to be heard.	He can't wait to hear you.
Your case will require going through gazillion red tapes.	The only red tape is your repentance.

The two thieves crucified alongside Jesus were both found guilty by the law of man, and were handed a verdict commensurate with their offenses. Hypothetically, they both received double death sentences—one from man (physical death) and the other from God (spiritual death). The one from man had them executed for their crimes. Apparently, they couldn't secure a commutation or termination of their death sentences. But there on the cross, one of them had his second death sentence commuted to life in paradise because he took the necessary steps to have it reversed. He realized his erring, admitted his guilt, and turned to the ultimate Life Saver for mercy.

If you repent of your sins and return to the Lord, you will be saved from spiritual death (Acts 3:19). Your appeal for mercy and pardon, made directly to the Judge of the earth (Genesis 18:25), results in immediate freedom from eternal damnation—no bonds posted, no payments made, no court appearances required, no lawyers hired, no witnesses called, no interrogations necessary, no jury selected, no delay of justice, no denial of mercy, and no language barrier. In whatever language you speak, repent of your sins, ask Jesus into your life as Lord and Savior, and your sentence too will be commuted to life in heaven.

In your pain and agony, turn to Christ for peace and harmony

It takes experience to know how something feels. Having been through different pains as a person, including labor pains, I know that pain is not pleasant. Be it physical, mental, emotional, or psychological, nobody embraces pain with delight. From some of the accounts I've read, crucifixion pain is the worst of all pains. We can only imagine what the three men—Jesus and the two thieves—endured.

But at a time of great agony, one of the thieves turned to the Savior. Instead of letting his pains make him blaspheme Christ—like the other thief did—he comported himself and asked Jesus to remember him in His kingdom. He refused to let his transitory pains rob him of a pain-free life in eternity (Revelation 21:4).

Everyone has a cross to carry. But some crosses are heavier than others because of the varying degrees of trial and suffering. Some believers are going through unthinkable faith-trying times. Lives that were going rosy are suddenly flooded by a torrent of thorns—joblessness, failed marriage, loss of loved one, collapsed business, unruly children, demotion, financial burden, bad health, accidents, loss of properties, etc. These thorns are real, and so is the pain they produce. Though believers in Christ, but things don't always work out the way we desire. And in the face of appalling disappointments, trials, suffering, heartaches, and hopelessness, it's easy to feel forsaken and abandoned by God, the same way Jesus felt on the cross.

But in our most frustrating moments, when our faith in God is dulled by fear, when we call and no answer, when there's no way forward and the enemy is closing in on us, when the cross gets too heavy to carry and no one cares to help, when our most trusted friends all leave and desert us, we can find peace and harmony if we turn to the Lord. There's nothing we may go through that He did not go through.

If you've experienced something in life, it's easier for you to relate to, and empathize with someone who's currently going through the same thing. And if you're passing through a season, you will prefer to talk to someone that passed through the same season and emerged victorious. That's exactly how Jesus is to all souls, saved or unsaved. He can relate to our pains because He experienced every form of pain that we will ever experience. The Bible says, "For we have not an high priest which cannot be touched with the feeling of our infirmities; but was in all points tempted like as we are, yet without sin" (Hebrews 4:15). We can turn to Him without fear of reprimand.

On the other hand, God can use situations in our lives to get our attention. Sometimes we're too focused on ourselves. We place more emphasis on provision than salvation. If we're rich, God is good. If not, God is unfair. We forget that God is more interested in our eternity than in any prosperity we can boast of. Our riches without our repentance is vanity in eternity.

Yes, God is "not willing that any should perish, but that all should come to repentance" (2 Peter 3:9). But He still needs our cooperation to roll away the stone of death for a life of joy; to put the rod to the water, so we can walk over to our victory; to release our ashes to Him, so we can enjoy His beauty. Why not turn to Him now and do what the thief did on the cross? In your pain and agony, turn to Him and receive His peace and harmony.

Verbally declare your salvation

For with the heart man believeth unto righteousness; and with the mouth confession is made unto salvation.
Romans 10:10

Think of a criminal standing before a court Judge. The criminal is sorry about his (her) crimes. If the remorse is not voiced out, how will the Judge know? Either to plead for leniency, ask for forgiveness, or disagree with the verdict, the guilty must open his (her) mouth and talk. The only way to make his (her) mind known is to verbally communicate his (her) thoughts.

It's the same picture when a sinner stands before God, the Judge of the universe. Why would you stand mute before Him? Going back to the thief on the cross, it wasn't impossible for Christ to read his mind because He's Omniscient. But I believe there's a reason why "with the mouth confession is made unto salvation." With his mouth, the thief confessed unto his salvation by asking Jesus for mercy in front of a huge crowd.

Some people may not understand why you need to talk about your salvation. After all, it's your life and nobody else's. That's true. But verbalizing your salvation not only humbles you, it'll prevent you from falling back into sin because you know people will be watching you.

It also means you're not ashamed to publicly declare your stand with the Lord. The saved thief had every reason to be ashamed. It's very possible that some of his victims and relatives of dead victims (if any) were there at his execution. His friends and family members could be there too, but acted like they didn't know him because they were embarrassed. That should have made him keep his head bowed till he died.

Instead, he buried his shame, raised his head, turned to the Savior, opened his mouth, and asked Jesus to remember him in His kingdom. Had he let shame prevent him from uttering those words, he would have gone to hell. Don't be ashamed of the Lord or the gospel.

For whosoever shall be ashamed of me and of my words, of him shall the Son of man be ashamed, when he shall come in his own glory, and in his Father's, and of the holy angels.
Luke 9:26

For I am not ashamed of the gospel of Christ: for it is the power of God unto salvation to every one that believeth; to the Jew first, and also to the Greek.
Romans 1:16

If you've never verbally declared your stand for Christ, as Lord and Savior, please do so without shame or intimidation. Say the words and shame the devil.

Proximity has nothing to do with salvation

The saved criminal was right beside Jesus, and very, very close to Him. And that explains why he was saved. Right? Wrong!!! His close distance to Jesus had nothing to do with his salvation. The other criminal was also beside Jesus. Yet, he missed it because he made no move for repentance.

Judas was even closer to Jesus than the two thieves. He was with Jesus for three miracle-filled years, dining and wining at the same table with the Lord, sleeping in the same place with Him, and walking the dusty roads by His side. He was so physically close to the Lord, yet so spiritually distant from Him. In person, he was a disciple and follower of Christ. At heart, he was a thief and a traitor.

If distance were a factor in salvation, none of us born after Christ would be saved. He's in heaven, we're on earth. How farther away from Him can we be? Yet, souls get saved daily, over two thousand years and counting, after His resurrection. If you think you're too far from Him, I've got good news for you. He's much closer to you than you ever thought or imagined, either for Him to hear you or save you.

He says, "Behold, I stand at the door and knock. If anyone hears my voice and opens the door, then I will come in to him, and will dine with him, and he with me" (Revelation 3:20, WEB). He's knocking on the door of your heart, waiting for you to let Him come into your life. I doubt if He can be any closer than that.

Regardless of how far you have strayed from the Lord, the only thing standing between you and Jesus is your repentance. No sinner can be too far from being saved. Satan will try any ploy to make you miss heaven. But it's up to you to place him where he belongs, under your feet. Step on him and use him as a ladder to the Father.

Seize the moment

The penitent thief knew he was going to die and he took advantage of the little time he had left to secure his salvation, while he was still alive and alert. But not everyone will be that opportune to get saved at the last minute. The Bible stipulates both the accepted time and day of salvation as, *now.*

Behold, now is the accepted time; behold, now is the day of salvation.
2 Corinthians 6:2

Since no one knows the time of death, it's best to repent and receive forgiveness before it's too late. Everyone prays to live long and fulfill their years on earth. But age has nothing to do with salvation. If you live longer than Methuselah (969 years, Genesis 5:27), it'll still be a wasted life if you die without Christ.

Procrastination is dangerous to your salvation. You may think you have it all figured out. You're strong, energetic, wealthy, smart, and whatever. And those are all good. In fact, those qualities can enhance long life. But if you think being all that guarantees long life, you're terribly mistaken. Like David said, there's only one step between us and death (1 Samuel 20:3).

Whereas we're masters over last moment, next moment is master over us, leaving us with nothing but *"now"* to seize. A second chance is good, but it's not guaranteed. That a person wakes up this morning is no guarantee that he (she) will make it to the night, or wake up tomorrow. Like in the days of Noah, many souls will go to hell because they neglect the opportunity to be saved.

As the days of Noah were, so will be the coming of the Son of Man. For as in those days which were before the flood they were eating and drinking, marrying and giving in marriage, until the day that Noah entered into the ship, and they didn't know until the flood came, and took them all away.
Matthew 24:37-39, WEB

Like every other thing in their lives, they procrastinated their salvation because they thought they got enough years ahead of them to enjoy life. And Satan quickly took advantage of their carelessness to blind their minds to the truth.

He hath blinded their eyes, and hardened their heart; that they should not see with their eyes, nor understand with their heart, and be converted, and I should heal them.
John 12:40

Please don't let that be said of you when your life is over. Don't waste another minute. The signs are all over the place that Christ's return is very imminent. His coming will be sudden, like the unexpected arrival of thieves in the night.

Watch therefore, for ye know neither the day nor the hour wherein the Son of man cometh.
Matthew 25:13

Remember therefore how thou hast received and heard, and hold fast, and repent. If therefore thou shalt not watch, I will come on thee as a thief, and thou shalt not know what hour I will come upon thee.

Revelation 3:3

Thieves don't announce when they will strike. They prefer to catch sleeping folks off-guard. That's how the coming of the Lord will be for the sleepy in spirit. If you don't want that to be your portion, *Carpe diem*...seize the moment.

Believe and you will be saved

In many ways, human nature relies on evidence to establish fact. Even in ordinary job search, some offices require donkey's years of experience before they can employ a person.

As the two thieves hung on their individual crosses, one repented, the other mocked. Hanging between them was Jesus, the Man many knew as the miracle worker. He healed sicknesses and drove out demons (Mark 1), turned water to wine (John 2), walked on water without drowning (Matthew 14), fed five thousand people with five loaves and two fishes (John 6), fed four thousand with seven loaves and a few small fish (Mark 8), and even commanded a dead-and-buried man out of the grave (John 11). Now hanging on the cross and He "cannot" save Himself.

To the unrepentant thief, all those miracle wonders were either made-up stories or the *man* used some evil power to deceive people. And whoever believed them must be living in an illusion of trust in a delusional human being. Even the Pharisees felt that way.

And all the people were amazed, and said, Is not this the son of David? But when the Pharisees heard it, they said, This fellow doth not cast out devils, but by Beelzebub the prince of the devils.
Matthew 12:23-24

Let's be honest. Action, they say, speaks louder than words. If you found yourself in the same situation as the unrepentant thief, would you not think the same thing? I don't know about you. But I doubt if I would have acted different before I got saved. And I know that many people, believers included, would have acted that way, too. But that kind of mindset contradicts what faith is all about. Faith simply means believe and you shall receive.

When the thief asked to be with Jesus in His kingdom, he already lost every itsy-bitsy, teeny-weeny desire for his life leading up to his crucifixion. He was tired, he was fed up, and he hated his life with a stronger passion than he used to love it. He had come to the end of the rope and he wanted something better, something different, something more promising, and desperately so. But why did he turn to Christ, who was also being crucified for His "crimes"? Well, he did because he saw Jesus by faith and not by sight. It was by faith that he asked Jesus to remember him in His kingdom.

The grace to be saved is a free gift to everyone, even the unrepentant thief. But it takes faith to believe and accept that grace, leading unto salvation. Just because the grace is free doesn't mean that salvation is automatic. When the keeper of prisons asked Paul and Silas, "Sirs, what must I do to be saved?" they replied, "Believe on the Lord Jesus Christ, and thou shalt be saved" (Acts 16:30-31). If you believe, you shall be saved (Matthew 21:22).

No sinner is beyond redemption

For God so loved the world, that he gave his only begotten Son, that whosoever believeth in him should not perish, but have everlasting life.
John 3:16

Whosoever is all inclusive, and it means any sinner can be restored and redeemed. A criminal that was already nailed to the cross asked to be with Jesus in His kingdom. And he got his wish because no sinner is a fiasco—a complete failure.

In Luke 15, Jesus tells the parable of the prodigal son, who left home for a far country where he squandered his portion of his father's possessions. When he returned home after a long absence, the father welcomed him with a banquet-like reception. The older son got mad because he didn't think his brother deserved to be received back into the house, much less celebrated. He missed the point: That the return of a sinner is victory over Satan, and it's worth celebrating. That's why heaven bursts into joy when a soul is saved (Luke 15:7).

It's hard to believe that someone like Paul would make heaven after masterminding the killing of so many innocent people. That guy detested Christians and he spared no energy persecuting, jailing, and killing any of them caught in the web of his blazing temperament and uncontrolled legalistic zeal for his Jewish beliefs. Those who professed faith in Christ were cruelly massacred, of which Stephen is the most popular (Acts 7:58; 8:1; 22:20). That's why some people, believers included, don't think it's fair that God could forgive such a savage.

But to err is human, to forgive is divine. The moment Paul surrendered his life to Christ, all his sins, which were as scarlet, were instantly forgiven and made "as white as snow" (Isaiah 1:18). If any of his victims were unsaved churchgoers, it means they missed heaven. Meanwhile, their killer got saved and made heaven.

Whereas the law of man brings physical death and condemnation to man, the love of God saves man from spiritual death and condemnation.

Same thing with the thief. We have no idea how many lives he sent to hell prior to his salvation on the cross. But before he died, he repented, was forgiven, and he will enjoy paradise with Jesus. How fair is that? Well, fair has nothing to do with salvation. What we think is completely our burden, not Christ's.

God is no respecter of persons: But in every nation he that feareth him, and worketh righteousness, is accepted with him.
Acts 10:34-35

God is not keeping a journal of your mistakes. No matter how messed up you are, He doesn't think of you as a mess. No matter how many times you have failed, He doesn't see you as a failure. The world may see you as useless, the Lord sees you as useful. To your friends, you are beyond rehabilitation. To the Lord, you can still be redeemed. You can experience that second chance free of strings. What others think of your life is inconsequential to what God wants to do with your life. Ignore any negative thoughts to make you feel your case is beyond pardon. No sinner is beyond redemption because there's no such thing as irreparable life. If that criminal could make heaven, so can any sinner that repents. Hey, if I could be saved, so can you.

I can just picture that thief getting to heaven, hugging the saints, and Jesus saying, *Look who I brought.* God doesn't care how many sins you've committed, or how bad a life you have lived. Just repent and ask Him to forgive you, and be sincere about it. And you too will be with Jesus in paradise.

Prayer of salvation: shortest, yet most important

The criminal's request to Jesus is the shortest salvation prayer that I know. No beating around the bush—just one simple, genuine, and straight-from-the-heart request. But encapsulated in that one-sentence prayer was his sincerity of purpose, admission of guilt, plea for forgiveness, recognition of the Lord's sovereignty, submission to the Lord's will, faith in the Lord's saving power, desire for the free grace, willingness to part with his sordid past, and readiness to spend eternity with Jesus.

From that point forward, a man that was declared missing and dead in God's kingdom, was rubber-stamped found and alive (Luke 15). A man that was an illegal alien in God's kingdom was instantly restored a legal citizen of heaven (Ephesians 2). The man who lived his entire life as Satan's servant instantly became God's son and joint-heir with Christ (Romans 8). Except the prayer of salvation, no other prayer encompasses all these life-saving and eternity-giving elements at once.

I'm not dismissing other prayers as unimportant. But if you think about it, you'll realize that something you consider important may not make the list on your twin's agenda. Part of the Lord's prayer asks us to pray for daily bread—food. For those living in famine-ravaged countries, hunger would force them to pray for food every day, if not every hour. But rich people have no reason to pray for food, because they have a steady supply, probably in excess. To a blind man, praying to receive sight is important, but not important to a deaf man with two good eyes. The differences in requests take the universality out of general prayers to God.

The prayer of salvation is the most important because it's universal and leaves no one out. Regardless of who you are, where you live, what you have, or how people perceive you, you were born a sinner (Psalm 51:5). And you must accept Christ as Lord and Savior, so you don't go to hell.

Not all are sick or need medication. But all are sinners and need salvation.

Are you ready to ask Jesus into your life? It's the most important prayer you will ever pray because your life after this earth depends on it. You don't have to use the exact same words the thief used on the cross. And you don't have to scratch your head for words either. Say what you can and God understands perfectly. Once you say that prayer and mean it with your heart, you have peace on earth and guaranteed bliss in heaven.

Be willing and determined to spend eternity with Jesus

A person that's willing and determined is more likely to complete tasks than someone who's willing, but not determined. I know some strong-willed individuals, who're very obdurate to other peoples' suggestions. Their *prima donna* attitude makes them very unteachable and hard to convince about anything contrary to their "always right" opinion. And that they care more about being right than they do about doing things right makes them particularly hard to get along with. But bad as that character trait is, it's a good quality to have when it comes to salvation.

A believer who tries to please everybody will have a tough time staying saved. No matter how good you are, once you profess to be saved, be ready for criticisms from cynics who detest your "nonsensical religiosity." And if you react to every negative and discouraging opinions of others, you will lose your salvation in no time. Don't let other people's perception of you cause you to miss the Lord's free offer of salvation to you.

The door of heaven is open to anyone willing to enter. And in my opinion, it's the easiest thing to do. Some people think that salvation has too many strings attached to it, too many dos and don'ts. Some even think of God as a despotic ruler, who forces His will on people without considering their thoughts or feelings. That's not so. We serve a loving God, Who sent His only Son Jesus Christ, to come and die for our sins, so we can live and not have to worry about the second death. Doing so makes salvation free for all. But it's still up to each person to either accept or reject the free gift.

Notice Jesus never said anything to the mocking thief? He knew that guy already made a choice for eternal perdition. On the contrary, the repentant thief felt the need to be saved because he wished to spend his after-life with Jesus. And the decision to ask came from him without duress from Jesus or anyone in the crowd. He could have kept his opinion to himself and nobody would have charged him for it. But because he was willing, he wasted no time asking.

Much as Jesus wishes for everyone to accept Him as Lord and Savior, He'll never force anyone to do so. But if anyone does, He'll never reject the person. Are you willing to spend eternity with Jesus? Then do what the thief did. With strong and sincere determination, ask Him to forgive you your sins and promise to serve Him till the end.

Foye Adedokun

Beware of distractions

The Bible says that "a great company of people" followed Jesus (Luke 23:27) from Pilate's palace. No doubt Golgotha was packed full on that day. Marching feet of crowd beyond control, clanging sounds of hammer on nails, mocking mouths and sobbing voices, sarcastic comments from ignorant spectators, some hands clapping, other hands patting. Add all that to the dissonant yelling from the crudely insensitive and brutish complicits of evil, whose voices were contorted with rage and violence. The noise on that hill would be nothing short of a thunderous uproar of bewildering cacophony.

With all that confusion on all sides, coupled with the pressure of hanging on the cross, no doubt the saved thief was surrounded by enough distractions. Yet, he tuned everything out to have a salvation dialogue with the only Man that mattered in the entire crowd—Jesus. His goal at that memorable moment was to secure eternal life. There was nothing he could do about his sad fate or the noise around him. But he didn't let that take his mind off the most important thing—his salvation.

Physical, emotional, or spiritual battles produce pains that are as real for believers as they are for unbelievers. And every battle in life is subject to tactical distractions, to make even the most determined valiant lose focus and miss the victory. There are unbelievers who truly wish to be saved. But they're faced with all kinds of dizzying pressure from friends and family, whose words are like daggers in the hearts of the hearers. Many give up when they can no longer stomach the disparaging comments and remarks. Some are wise enough to repent, but many die in that condition, without ever reconciling with the Savior.

Distractions can be frustrating to the point that a person, spirit-filled or not, loses his (her) temper and does something that he (she) later regrets, and the mistake may be too late to correct. Moses, after leading the Israelites out of Egyptian bondage, missed the Promised Land because he succumbed to distracting noises from the hard-to-please brood of whiners. Instead of speaking to the rock as instructed by God, he smote it because they provoked him (Numbers 20:2-11; Deuteronomy 34:4). What a lamentable experience that must have been for Moses.

The same fate would have befallen the saved thief if he had let those loud scenes distract him from the Savior. He would have missed the chance to enter paradise.

When you're ready to make amends or when you determine to accept Christ as your Lord and Savior, be ready for all kinds of distractions. I promise you they will come. But you must ignore them if you plan on succeeding. Disregard whatever pressures might be raging against you. Soon, you will testify of the Lord's goodness.

Foye Adedokun

Past life as a distraction

*Brethren, I count not myself to have apprehended: but this one
thing I do, forgetting those things which are behind, and reaching
forth unto those things which are before, I press toward the mark
for the prize of the high calling of God in Christ Jesus.*
Philippians 3:13-14

Of all the distractions a penitent sinner has to deal with,
past life is the hardest to overcome. We all make mistakes; and
when we realize them, we make things right. But even when a
person is truly sorry, some aspects of the past cannot be undone.
When bombarded with guilt over sins committed years ago, it
can hinder repentance attempt. Each time the person takes a step
forward, he (she) takes two steps back when Satan reminds him
(her) of that horrible incident. In some cases, when a person
summons enough courage to forget his (her) past, other people will
remind him (her) of how awful he (she) used to be.

Before his conversion, Paul terrorized and killed Christians
who didn't share his Jewish beliefs. But after his conversion, he
realized his ignorance.

*I am verily a man which am a Jew, born in Tarsus, a city in Cilicia,
yet brought up in this city at the feet of Gamaliel, and taught
according to the perfect manner of the law of the fathers, and was
zealous toward God, as ye all are this day.*
Acts 22:3 (Emphasis mine)

I would think that somebody that highly learned would be more inclined to tolerate other faiths. But his level of education only deepened his ignorance of the real truth. The whole time he "persecuted this way unto the death, binding and delivering into prisons both men and women" (Acts 22:4), he thought he was being zealous for God. Can you then imagine his guilt when he became a member of the same body he persecuted for so long?

Naturally, when news spread of his conversion, some folks didn't believe (Acts 9:10-14, 19-21). In fact, when he went to Jerusalem and tried to join the disciples, the Bible says, "they were all afraid of him, not believing that he was a disciple" (Acts 9:26, WEB). If disciples were afraid of him, others must have been frightened just hearing his name.

I wouldn't be surprised if no one believed or paid attention to his first sermon after his conversion. His mere presence evoked fear. And for those that had encountered his cruel wrath before, seeing him again would seem like a *déjà vu* of a deadly attack from a man who was only using honied words to lure them into his dangerous trap. It probably took some time after his conversion before Paul finally overcame the stigma of his past life.

Today, many souls are dealing with guilt and stigma over their past life. Each time they struggle to put it behind them, Satan reopens their drying wounds of guilt, making it impossible for complete healing to take place.

On the repentant thief, the devil lost any attempt to prevent him from getting saved. There's no mention of his age, how long he had been a thief, or the exact crime that led him to the cross. Perhaps he was a *recidivist*, constantly and habitually relapsing into crimes, not minding how many times he was caught and punished. No idea, except he must have committed a terrible crime to warrant an execution. But by asking to be with Jesus in His kingdom, he put his past where it belonged—in the past—so he could enjoy a glorious future with the Lord.

You need to let go of those guilty feelings that have kept you from taking the next step toward your salvation. God has promised to blot out your transgressions and remember them no more (Isaiah 43:24). If He doesn't remember your sins, you don't need to remember them. Don't you have other things to do? Put your past behind you so you can experience the joy of being saved and forgiven. The thief did, Paul did, I did, and you can, too.

Jesus is never too occupied to hear you

From Gethsemane to the time Jesus was nailed to the cross, it was one bad moment leading to a more terrible moment.

Then cometh Jesus with them unto a place called Gethsemane, and saith unto the disciples, Sit ye here, while I go and pray yonder. And he took with him Peter and the two sons of Zebedee, and began to be sorrowful and very heavy. Then saith he unto them, My soul is exceeding sorrowful, even unto death.
Matthew 26:36-38

After His arrest, He was tortured all the way to Golgotha where He was crucified in a most dehumanizing manner. With nails hammered into His hands and feet, the agony of crucifixion made Him cry, "My God, my God, why hast thou forsaken me?" (Matthew 26:46). With that horrible pain and the deafening clanging noise all over the place, the Lord should have been too uptight to notice anyone trying to get His attention, or hear anything being whispered to Him. But not our Savior. His pain didn't numb His mind to the desperate request of a sober sinner.

There were various instances when individuals approached Him while surrounded by crowd. As busy as He was—casting out demons, healing sicknesses and diseases, feeding thousands with little, and even restoring life back into the dead—He never failed to give that individual attention to those who came to Him. Even when He appeared to snub them, He still granted their desires.

- In the coasts of Tyre and Sidon, when a woman came crying unto Him on behalf of her daughter who was "grievously vexed with a devil" (Matthew 15:21-28).

- In Cana of Galilee, when His mother approached Him for more wine on behalf of the wedding guests (John 2:1-8).

- In Capernaum, when a woman touched the hem of His garment and she was instantly healed of a twelve-year blood hemorrhage (Luke 8:43-48).

- In Jericho, when a height-deprived Zacchaeus climbed a tree to catch a glimpse of Him. Jesus sensed his desperate move, looked up, and asked him to, "make haste, and come down; for to day I must abide at thy house" (Luke 19:1-9).

- In Bethany, when Mary and Martha sent for Him while their brother—Lazarus—was only sick, but Jesus showed up four days later, after Lazarus was already dead and buried (John 11:1-44).

- In Jericho, when blind Bartimaeus, the highway-side beggar, heard of Jesus passing and cried out to Him for mercy (Mark 10:46-52).

When you decide to know Him, no condition can stop Him from wanting to know you. When you express a desire to follow Him, He will gladly receive you. When you ask Him to remember you in His kingdom, He will readily grant your wish. On the mountain, in the valley, on the cross, on a tree, on land, or in the deep mighty ocean, call on Him and He'll answer you.

When Jesus acquits, no man can accuse

People are quick to remind us (or God) of our shortcomings. There are people out there who know more about you, or think they know more about you, than you know about yourself. And since they don't care about eternity anyway, they will find any reason to make you feel guilty about your life. Recounting your sins and offenses gives them some fleeting gratification because it makes them feel they're better than you.

Again, let's take a look at the reaction of the prodigal son's brother when he returned home.

Now his elder son was in the field. As he came near to the house, he heard music and dancing. He called one of the servants to him, and asked what was going on. He said to him, 'Your brother has come, and your father has killed the fattened calf, because he has received him back safe and healthy.' But he was angry, and would not go in. Therefore his father came out, and begged him. But he answered his father, 'Behold, these many years I have served you, and I never disobeyed a commandment of yours, but you never gave me a goat, that I might celebrate with my friends. But when this, your son, came, who has devoured your living with prostitutes, you killed the fattened calf for him.'
Luke 15:25-30, WEB

He saw everything wrong with his little brother, and saw nothing wrong with himself. But his accusations had no effect on the father's decision to forgive his errant son and restore him back into his bosom.

When the penitent thief asked Christ to remember him in His kingdom, he received instant redemption and forgiveness of sins. After that, not a peep from anyone in the crowd. Nobody, not even the soldiers, dared to challenge that paradise pact between the Christ and the criminal. If they did, it wasn't significant enough for the Bible to record it. Christ said it and that sealed it. On the judgment day, that thief will stand before the judgment throne just as if he never sinned.

If the Son therefore shall make you free, ye shall be free indeed.
John 8:36

Once Jesus says you're free, you are F-R-E-E. Not partially, not so-so, not perhaps, but totally and unconditionally free. If He acquits you, no one can accuse you or bring up your case before Him anymore. If someone is not happy about it, let it remain the person's headache, not yours. If God be for you, no one can be against you (Romans 8:31).

Salvation transcends religious protocol

I believe in good works. And I seriously doubt the salvation of anyone who claims to be a Christian but acts nonchalant, either toward others or the ordinances of God. A born-again person must show forth fruits that give credence to genuine salvation. However, we must be careful not to think any less of people who die shortly after getting saved, with no chance to fulfill all righteousness.

Before going further, let's consider some things a newly saved Christian is expected to do to make his salvation pure and complete, and see if the saved thief accomplished any of them between the time he was saved and the time he died.

a. Ask forgiveness from his victims

Leading up to his crucifixion, that thief led a criminal life. Then, so cheaply, he turned to Jesus, made one statement, and, *bam*, he obtained the paradise visa—no application forms, no fees, no interview, no background checks, no fingerprinting, no civics test. Are you kidding me? I can't even obtain a Nigerian visa that easy.

And how about his victims? Though possible that nobody offended him, it was impossible that he offended nobody. Other-wise, to dub him a criminal or a thief would be a documented biblical blunder. There must be some individuals in that village whose lives were negatively impacted by his crimes. He was supposed to secure their forgiveness before he died. Since he failed to do that, it's so unfair that Jesus forgave him. And he shouldn't be in heaven or anywhere near its gate.

I won't be surprised if someone feels that way. Definitely a true believer should secure the forgiveness of people he (she) has offended. But time failed the saved thief to accomplish that goal. Yet, he made heaven.

b. Baptism in water

When Peter finished his firestorm sermon on the day of Pentecost, those who received and believed the Word asked what they must do to be saved. Peter replied, "Repent, and be baptized every one of you in the name of Jesus Christ for the remission of sins, and ye shall receive the gift of the Holy Ghost" (Acts 2:38).

Before Jesus began His ministry, John baptized Him in the Jordan river (Matthew 3:13-17). And while commissioning His disciples after His resurrection, Jesus asks them to "Go, and make disciples of all nations, baptizing them in the name of the Father and of the Son and of the Holy Spirit" (Matthew 28:19, WEB), further proving the importance of baptism.

Water baptism is one of the much-talked-about topics in the church because the Bible commands baptism after repentance. As a Christian, I believe in baptism. I've been baptized twice, both by full immersion. The first wasn't genuine because I only followed the crowd, not my personal conviction. I even took up an English name because the pastor said it was the right thing to do. After all, how could I claim to be Baptist and not have an English name? So,

I picked Stella because I liked the sound of it. And from that point forward, I lived as the sinful Stella without giving any thoughts to my actions.

Seven years later, the Holy Spirit convinced me to repeat the process. March 1987, married and six months pregnant with first child, I had a second but genuine baptism by immersion in a flowing river, in the proper order of identifying with the death and resurrection of my Lord and Savior Jesus Christ, buried and risen with Him "through the faith of the operation of God, who hath raised him from the dead" (Colossians 2:12), to live forever dead to sin, never again to go the way of the world (Romans 6:1-4).

I said all that to show my full support for baptism, but not to imply that baptism is required for salvation to be complete. A person may be baptized trillion times and still go to hell. But, like the saved thief, time may hinder a convert—new or returning—from getting baptized before death, and the person will still make heaven. The thief had a chance for repentance, but time failed him for baptism. Yet, he made heaven.

c. Fellowshipping with other believers

When Phillip encountered the Ethiopian eunuch, Phillip asked if he understood what he was reading on prophet Esaias. The eunuch replied, "How can I, except some man should guide me?" (Acts 8:31).

To nurture his (her) soul, and for a better understanding of

God's Word, a new convert should fellowship with other believers. However, missing the grace to do so won't hinder the convert's eternity with Jesus. For lack of time after his salvation, the thief could not fellowship with other believers. But because he had Christ, he made heaven.

d. Praying daily and studying the Bible

I remember this song from Sunday school.

Read your Bible, pray every day
Pray every day, pray every day
Read your Bible, pray every day
And you'll grow, grow, grow.

Just as food and water give us vitality for physical growth and survival, prayer and meditation give us vitality for spiritual growth. A believer that fails to pray and meditate is a spiritual dwarf. For any reason and perhaps to thank Jesus for saving him, the thief might have said a silent prayer, unheard by anyone. But he never got the chance to pray and meditate every day because his life terminated on the cross. Yet, he would be with Jesus in paradise.

e. Restitution (See page 43 for more on restitution.)

Restitution is the act of returning or paying for items that are mistakenly, falsely, or forcibly taken from rightful owners. As a tax collector, Zacchaeus made people pay more taxes than due. But after his encounter with Jesus, he pledged half of his goods to the poor and a fourfold restitution of anything he took from people "by false accusation" (Luke 19:8). That was a genuine restitution.

Today, criminals get saved in prisons. But if they don't get the chance to restitute, or the restitution is impossible—like a murder case—their salvation will still be honored in heaven. Like the saved thief, they will escape eternity in hell fire and will reign with Jesus in paradise.

For him, robbing others to survive was his chosen career. But after getting saved on the cross, he had no chance either to return stolen items still in his possession, or pay their monetary value. Yet he made heaven. And there's nothing anyone can do about it.

f. Soul winning

The salvation of a soul only happens through the convicting power of the Holy Spirit. But from what Jesus said to His disciples, we know He wants believers to tell others about Him.

But you will receive power when the Holy Spirit has come upon you. You will be witnesses to me in Jerusalem, in all Judea and Samaria, and to the uttermost parts of the earth.
Acts 1:8, WEB

A saved person is expected to disciple other people to the kingdom by telling them about Jesus Christ. But there was no way the thief could have done that within the time frame between getting saved and giving up the ghost. Yet, he made heaven.

271

Foye Adedokun

g. Tithing

Few years back, a member of our former church came to our house to convince us against tithing. He said that tithing is voluntary and nothing spiritual about it. Somehow, I fell for it, but not for long before the Holy Spirit rebuked me. Tithing is a biblical principle.

Will a man rob God? Yet ye have robbed me. But ye say, Wherein have we robbed thee? In tithes and offerings. Ye are cursed with a curse: for ye have robbed me, even this whole nation. Bring ye all the tithes into the storehouse, that there may be meat in mine house, and prove me now herewith, saith the Lord of hosts, if I will not open you the windows of heaven, and pour you out a blessing, that there shall not be room enough to receive it.
Malachi 3:8-10

A true Christian should pay tithes. But a person who dies shortly after getting saved may never get the chance to pay tithes. And I know he (she) will still make heaven, no questions asked. There was no time left for the saved thief to pay tithes after his on-the-cross salvation. Yet, he made heaven.

h. Walking with the Lord

When I had my first child, I knew I could no longer live the way I did before I became a mother, something I looked forward to. But I gladly embraced the challenges that came with my joy, like sleepless nights, adjusting my schedule to make room for my baby, or packing more stuff than needed for every trip.

The Bible says, "As ye have therefore received Christ Jesus the Lord, so walk ye in him" (Colossians 2:6). Once a person is saved and born again into the family of God, his (her) way of life must change, including conversation, lifestyle, and principles. But that's easier for some people than others, depending on the extent of the damages they've caused themselves and others. And relative to that thief, it would be loads of changes to make.

Did he get the chance to do that? No, because time failed him. Yet, he made heaven.

Unless you're in the same or similar situation as the saved thief—with no chance after repentance—you have no excuse for religious laxity. If you're truly saved, obligation calls on you to fulfill all righteousness and do good works (James 2:18-20). To have the time to fulfill any of the listed works, and more, but fail to do so amounts to willful negligence. On the other hand, to dismiss the salvation of a sinner who misses the chance to perform any of those obligations as incomplete, is to assert that the atoning death of Christ alone, without the fulfillment of religious works, cannot suffice for the redemption of that sinner.

For by grace are ye saved through faith; and that not of yourselves: it is the gift of God: Not of works, lest any man should boast.
Ephesians 2:8-9

Jesus rebuked the Scribes and Pharisees as hypocrites, who "make clean the outside of the cup and of the platter, but within they are full of extortion and excess." He compared them "unto whited sepulchres, which indeed appear beautiful outward, but are within full of dead men's bones, and of all uncleanness," and "outwardly appear righteous unto men, but within ye are full of hypocrisy and iniquity" (Matthew 23:25, 27-28). That a person fulfills all the laws doesn't imply he (she) is truly saved, or even saved at all.

That criminal was a bad dude all the way to his execution. Humanly speaking, he didn't deserve such an easy pass to heaven. And neither do I. Yet, Christ forgave him, and forgave me, too. But whereas I've been blessed with years to fulfill the post-salvation protocols, he wasn't so fortunate. Regardless, he'll be my senior in eternity. He had no business with anybody, except Christ, his Savior. He owed no religious fanatics any explanation. He already settled his case with the Lord. The Lord already approved him. And if anyone is not pleased with that, let the person tell it to the Lord, or forever hold his (her) peace.

Salvation: a unique and personal experience

But the other answering rebuked him, saying, Dost not thou fear God, seeing thou art in the same condemnation? And we indeed justly; for we receive the due reward of our deeds: but this man hath done nothing amiss. And he said unto Jesus, Lord, remember me when thou comest into thy kingdom.
Luke 23:40-42 (Emphases mine)

Two criminals were crucified alongside Jesus. One was saved because he asked Jesus to remember him in His kingdom. But please read that cross dialogue again and note the language. In admission of guilt while rebuking the other thief, the saved thief said, **we.** When he asked Jesus to remember him in His kingdom, the conversation turned personal—**me.**

He already admitted they were both guilty and deserving of the punishment meted out to them. But, instead of asking Jesus to remember him, why not ask Jesus to remember both of them in His kingdom? The answer is simple. There's no such thing as group salvation. You and your friends can carpool to places, but you cannot *crosspool* to heaven. A soul, a cross.

When an altar call is made during any Christian gathering, hundreds may turn out to indicate their willingness to accept Christ. So, it's possible that you respond to an altar call with a group of people. If you get saved, it doesn't mean that everyone in the group is automatically saved. If hundred people come out and only two are sincerely repentant, heaven will only recognize those two.

The Bible says, "For God so loved the world, that he gave his only begotten Son, that whosoever believeth in him should not perish, but have everlasting life" (John 3:16). *Whosoever* means *anyone*, not *any group*. Each salvation experience is unique and personal, and each soul is responsible for his (her) walk with Christ. That's why preachers ask people to individually confess their sins.

Even if the repentant thief had asked the Lord to remember both of them, the prayer would not avail for the other thief if he didn't repent of his sins and accept Christ as Lord and Savior. No matter how close you are to a saved soul, your salvation totally rests with you. And no matter how close you are to an unsaved soul, your salvation is not their free ticket to heaven. Every soul bears its own cross. Salvation, though may be free for all, but each person still has to ask because at the judgment throne, each person will give an account of himself (herself) to God (Romans 14:12).

There's life after death

Four days after a man was certified dead by two doctors in two different hospitals, he sneezed back to life, with tears in his eyes. From the account of his experience during those four days, two things stood out—heaven and hell. He made it through the first gate to the second gate that led to the judgment seat in heaven.

He said heaven is so beautiful and he pleaded with the angel to let him proceed to the final gate. But the angel asked him to return because brethren here below wouldn't stop praying. On his way back, the angel led him past hell, where, from a very, very, long distance, he felt the heat from an inferno, a fire like a raging sea of red and yellow lava. Inside the fire was a tsunami of people, whose cries of pain and agony were deafening beyond earthly description.

Comparing his testimony with the Luke 16 account of the rich man and Lazarus the beggar, I believe everything that he saw. And the corroboration of both accounts make the subject of life after death more realistic and certain.

Now there was a certain rich man, and he was clothed in purple and fine linen, living in luxury every day. A certain beggar, named Lazarus, was laid at his gate, full of sores, and desiring to be fed with the crumbs that fell from the rich man's table. Yes, even the dogs came and licked his sores. The beggar died, and he was carried away by the angels to Abraham's bosom. The rich man also died, and was buried. In Hades, he lifted up his eyes, being in torment, and saw Abraham far off, and Lazarus at his bosom. He cried and said, 'Father Abraham, have mercy on me, and send Lazarus, that he may dip the tip of his finger in water, and cool my tongue! For I am in anguish in this flame.' "But Abraham said, 'Son, remember that you, in your lifetime, received your good things, and Lazarus, in the same way, bad things. But now here he is comforted and you are in anguish. Besides all this, between us and you there is a great gulf fixed, that those who want to pass from here to you are not able, and that no one may cross over from there to us.'

Luke 16:19-26, WEB

I'm convinced beyond any doubt that life doesn't end at death. Heaven is real, and so is hell. And the simple reply that Jesus gave the penitent thief on the cross further reinforces that fact. There's a good life after death and there's a bad life after death. The good life after death is with Jesus in heaven, the place where forgiven sinners go. The bad life after death is with Satan in hell, the place reserved for those that fail to repent of their sins, and never ask Jesus into their lives as Lord and Savior.

When the eyes of the saved thief closed on the cross, they would reopen in paradise. When your eyes are closed in death, where will they reopen—in heaven with Jesus or in hell with Satan? Please, don't believe any teaching that says your life ends at death. Secure your place now in Abraham's bosom. Ask Jesus into your heart, so you too can be with Him in eternity.

6

Where Will You Spend Eternity?

And as it is appointed unto men once to die, but after this the judgment.
Hebrews 9:27

Without the sin-cleansing power in the blood of our Lord Jesus Christ, His enemies would have done anything to ensure that any documentation of His suffering and crucifixion is reduced to only an ephemeral historical account. But believers know that everything that took place on Calvary revolved around Him and none of it can be denied. There was beating, pain, sorrow, bloodshed, anguish, confusion, and a feeling of abandonment. And if one were to think of the things that Christ suffered on Golgotha, tears of grief would flow unprovoked even at the most silent whisper of the word, *Cross*.

But that's not how He wants His followers to feel. Grieving for Him defeats the purpose of His suffering. He bore the heavy cross to lighten our own crosses. He endured the crucifixion to lighten our affliction. He died so we can live. And He wants us to take glory in nothing but the cross (Galatians 6:14).

279

But here's the warning. He didn't do all that to give us a free pass to heaven. Everyone will die, and everyone will spend eternity in one of two places—heaven or hell. Which brings me to the most important question. **Where will you spend eternity?**

Each morning when you wake up, you prepare for the day, double-checking items on your to-do list. Sometimes you prepare months or even years in advance of a plan because you hate to be disappointed. Are you that prepared for eternity? Have you ever considered what will happen when you die? Your life on earth is temporary and it's certain to end one day. Then you'll start another life that will never end. But your destination for that life depends on your decision in this life.

Some people think they will call on Jesus when at the brink of death, just like the thief did on the cross. They forget that there's no assurance they will be that fortunate. Sure the Bible says, "For whosoever shall call upon the name of the Lord shall be saved" (Romans 10:13). But that's not to suggest that every deliberate procrastination of salvation can be undone at the last minute. The thief was able to do what he did because he was fully conscious.

Death is a leveler. Regardless of age, status, height, color, culture, or creed, we all owe it to death and eternity.

None of us is promised the next moment, as death can strike at any time. And when death bids you come, you're going. Even if something happens and you're still breathing, you must be

280

conscious and have control over your mind to seek repentance.

Eternity is not about religion or denomination, but about repentance and salvation. Good thing you've been attending church since the day you were born. But unless you're saved, you cannot spend eternity with Christ. And no excuse for rejecting Him will suffice when you face the judgment throne.

Just think of it this way. If Christ loved you so much as to die for you, why would you love yourself any less? All He's asking is that you turn your attention to Him and ask to spend eternity with Him in His kingdom. Why's that so hard? Please give serious consideration to your eternal destiny. Let the thought continuously echo in your heart that eternity means time without end. The door of eternity only has an entry, no exit—once in, never out.

Don't let death usher you into eternal burden. Give your life to Christ and acknowledge Him as your Lord and Savior, so when your life on earth is over, you will be ushered into God's glorious presence to enjoy eternity basking in the splendor of His majesty. Don't waste time. Now is the accepted time and today is the day of salvation (2 Corinthians 6:2).

Foye Adedokun

In a nutshell

- God loved us so much He sent His Only Son, Jesus, to come and die for us. Anyone who believes in Him will have everlasting life (John 3:16).

- God did not send Jesus, so sinners can be condemned, but so sinners can be saved (John 3:17).

- Christ came as the Lamb of God to take away the sins of the world (John 1:29).

- If you receive Him and believe on His name, you will become a child of God (John 1:12).

- If you believe Him, you will not perish, but have eternal life (John 3:15).

- Jesus will, unconditionally, receive anyone who comes to Him and will forgive any sinner who confesses and repents of his (her) sins (John 6:37; 1 John 1:9).

- Jesus is in heaven preparing mansions for those who believe and accept Him as Lord and Savior (John 14:2-3).

- The only Way to God is Jesus Christ (John 14:6).

- You have one life to live. After that, you face God's judgment (Hebrews 9:27).

- If you're saved, be careful so you don't fall back into sins (1 Corinthians 10:12).

- Accept Christ today. Tomorrow may be too late (Hebrews 3:7).

- God wants everyone to come unto Him because He doesn't want anyone to perish (2 Peter 3:9).

- Delay is dangerous, for no one knows the time or hour when the end will come (Revelation 3:3).

- Your good works cannot save you, only grace through faith (Ephesians 2:8-9).

- If wealth can save, the rich man would not have gone to hell (Luke 16).

- If status can save, Jesus wouldn't have told Nicodemus, "You must be born again" (John 3).

- If possessions can save, the rich young ruler wouldn't have left Jesus' presence sorrowful (Luke 18).

- If knowledge or religious zeal can save, Paul should not have been converted. He had enough knowledge and zeal to be a Field Marshall in the army of God (Acts 9 & 22).

- If power can save, Nebuchadnezzar would not acknowledge the God of Shadrach, Meshach, and Abednego as, "the Most High" (Daniel 3).

- If delegated authority can save, the jailer would not ask Paul and Silas, "Sirs, what must I do to be saved?" (Acts 16:30).

- If riches can save, Solomon wouldn't describe his unsurpassed grandeur as "vanity of vanities. All is vanity" (Ecclesiastes 1).

- If the blood of bulls and goats can save, Jesus wouldn't have shed His blood for the remission of sins (Hebrews 10:4).

- If you're not sure if God loves you, remember He gave His Son to die for your sins.

- If you're not sure how much Jesus loves you, remember His death on the cross.

- If you think your life now is the worst, remember the thief on the cross. He was a criminal.

- If you think it must be difficult to get saved, remember the thief on the cross. He got saved just by asking Jesus to remember him in His kingdom.

- If you don't want to be the only one getting saved in a crowd, remember the thief on the cross. No record of another salvation in the midst of the huge Calvary crowd.

- If you're ashamed to ask Jesus into your life in public, remember the thief on the cross. He asked while hanging in front of an overwhelming crowd of spectators.

- If you think that a person's outward appearance has to do with the salvation of his (her) soul, remember the thief on the cross. His appearance couldn't have been the best.

- If you think you must kneel before an altar to confess your sins before you can be saved, remember the thief on the cross. He was saved while hanging on a cross.

- If you think only good people can be saved, remember the thief on the cross. He was a thief.

- If you think belonging to a certain denomination is a must for salvation, remember the thief on the cross. He probably didn't even belong to a church, much less a denomination.

- If you're waiting for someone to make the move before you do, remember the thief on the cross. He made the move without waiting for anybody.

- If you think salvation is not important, remember the thief on the cross. It must be important enough for a criminal to consider it.

- If you think your life is terrible beyond redemption, remember the thief on the cross. His terrible life earned him execution by crucifixion.

- If you've made life miserable for others and guilty conscience won't let you take a positive step forward, remember the thief on the cross. Considering the severity of his punishment, he must have made life a living hell for others.

- If you care what people may think if you repent, remember the thief on the cross. When he turned to Jesus for mercy, he could care less what anybody thought.

- If you care what your buddy will think if you accept Christ, remember the thief on the cross. He asked to be with Jesus without paying any attention to his criminal buddy.

- If you think you can only accept Christ after hearing a sermon from a preacher, remember the thief on the cross. There's no record of any sermon preached to him before he turned to Christ.

- If you think salvation can only occur during a religious service, remember the thief on the cross. The only service that took place on Golgotha was disservice to the Savior of the world.

- If you're prone to distractions that may affect your salvation, remember the thief on the cross. The noise and all the activities didn't stop him from turning to the only Man that mattered in the crowd—Jesus.

- If you think the Man who didn't save Himself from crucifixion can't save you, remember the thief on the cross. He didn't let what he saw affect what he sought.

- If you think accepting Christ now will avail nothing because you have no time left to fulfill religious obligations, remember the thief on the cross. He was saved on the cross and he died on the cross.

- If you're waiting for your pain to cease before asking Jesus into your life, remember the thief on the cross. When he turned to Jesus, his hands and feet were already nailed to the cross.

- If you think Jesus should automatically offer you eternal life without your asking, remember the thief on the cross. He asked before he received.

- If you think salvation prayer should be said with your eyes closed, remember the thief on the cross. I doubt if he closed his eyes while asking Jesus to remember him in His kingdom.

- If you're hours or minutes away from death, but can still think right, do what the thief did on the cross. His time on the cross was all he had, and he made good use of it.

- If you don't know how to avoid the deadly consequences of a sinful life, do what the thief did on the cross. Repent.

- If you don't want to spend eternity in hell fire, do what the thief did on the cross. Repent.

- When you don't know what to make of your life, do what the thief did on the cross. Turn to Jesus.

- When all else fails and you have no one to turn to, do what the thief did on the cross. Turn to Jesus.

- If you don't know how to pray a salvation prayer, say what the thief said on the cross.

- If that's too long for you to remember, just say, JESUS, forgive my sins.

For ages, the devil has been lying to billions of souls that they cannot make heaven. But join me and many others to shame him as we declare, *Sí, se puede...Yes, we can.* If I go before you, looking forward to welcoming you to heaven. If you go before me, looking forward to meeting you in heaven.

And until then, may the Lord bless you and keep you. May He make His face to shine upon you and be gracious unto you. May He lift up His countenance upon you and give you peace, in Jesus' Mighty Name. Amen.

BOOKS BY FOYE ADEDOKUN

Once Upon a Calvary: the Cross, the Christ, the Criminals (Paperback and Kindle).

There's No Place Like Home: The Return Journey of a Penitent Prodigal (Paperback and Kindle).

Copies may be obtained from:
http://www.amazon.com
http://amazon.co.uk

Made in the USA
Middletown, DE
27 August 2022

71964414R00176